God's Divine Help

146 Old & New Testament Devotions for Godly Living

By

Kenneth M. Lee

God's Divine Help by Kenneth Marshall Lee: Printed and bound in the United States of America. All composition rights by author are reserved. Material included herein shall not be used by any other person for commercial intent; neither shall it be reproduced for or within information storage and retrieval systems other than for the author's express use; however, material can be copied and used for the purpose of spiritual learning.

Copyright © 2017Klee

Library Control Number: 2017903759
Religion/Devotional

ISBN 978-0-9711850-4-3

About the Author: Kenneth M. Lee is a free-lance author who lives in Loris, South Carolina, U.S.A.
His devotions have been published in *The Loris Scene, Upper Room, Penned from the Heart, and The Secret Place.*
Other books by Kenneth Lee: *Devotions A-Z, God's Divine Way; Persecuted But Not Forsaken; Victim's Vengeance; Unveiled.*

His *Petition to Cease and Ban Direct Energy Programs and Surveillance of Humans* in 2004 brought together a group of covertly abused victims to seek justice.

www.thedivineway.wordpress.com

All Bible Scripture References are from the King James Version and the New Schofield Reference Edition of the Holy Bible.

Thy word is a lamp unto my feet, and a light unto my path.

            Psalms 119: 105

Preface

God's Divine Help originated when I saw a need for quick Biblical answers rather than having to search randomly through the Bible.

I summarized 73 subjects with Biblical precepts; and put a devotion with an Old Testament scripture and a devotion with a pertinent New Testament scripture.

God's Divine Help is not some kind of technical theological book, but I can assure you it evolved through deep prayer: I had experienced nearly every subject and the Lord put a burden on my soul to write about them.

For further research, I suggest acquiring an exhaustive concordance to the Bible, Hebrew and Greek Interlinear texts, an expository of Old and New Testament words, and other translations of the Holy Scriptures to ascertain God's truth.

But all the studying in the world will not enable a person to find complete rest, peace, and happiness, in a world polluted with weaponry, mass communication devices, and toxins. Until these devices are eliminated and toxins cleaned of land, sea, and air, there will be little environmental peace. Worse, human behavior can now be remotely manipulated through the use of artificial energy.

Yet God has commanded us to be holy; neither shall we defile the land.

As a young boy, taught by my Cherokee Indian bred mother, being holy, righteous, and reverent towards God, man, and the environment went a long way towards finding peace and happiness. Learning about the herbs of the field and their natural remedies helped keep me physically well.

But having a full relationship with God the Father in Heaven is the ultimate answer for complete joy.

May God reveal himself to you in *God's Divine Help*. May he grant you the peace, wisdom, and happiness that comes from knowing him and living in the Holy Spirit.

There is no greater joy -- than to serve the living God in truth, righteousness, love, and humble adoration.

Table of Contents

Abandoned	1
Adultery	3
Afraid	5
Aging	7
Alcohol	9
Anger	11
Argument	13
Believe	15
Building	17
Children	19
Confession	21
Confidence	23
Confusion	25
Courage	27
Crying	29
Death	31
Debt	33
Devil	35
Disability	37
Discouragement	39
Divorce	41
Drugs	43
Eating	45
Enemies	47
Evil	49
Faith	51
Fellowship	53
Forgiveness	55
Friends	57
Gambling	59
Homeless	61
Humble	63
Imprisonment	65
Jealousy	67
Joyfulness	69
Loneliness	71

Lost	73
Love	75
Lying	77
Marriage	79
Mercy	81
Money	83
Obedience	85
Patience	87
Peace	89
Persecution	91
Prayer	93
Pride	95
Purpose	97
Rejected	99
Repentance	101
Righteousness	103
Safety	105
Salvation	107
Secrets	109
Sexual Relations (Married)	111
Sexual Relations (Unmarried)	113
Sickness	115
Sin	117
Sports	119
Strength	121
Stress	123
Suicide	125
Terror	127
Thankfulness	129
Travel	131
Trials	133
Truth	135
War	137
Wisdom	139
Worry	141
Work	143
Worship	145

Abandoned – Old Testament

And they took him, and cast him into a pit, and the pit was empty; there was no water in it.
Genesis 37: 24

Joseph was abandoned by his brothers and left in a pit to die until some merchantmen came along to lift him out.

Friends or family may abandon us, or even try to sell us, but being abandoned is a good time for drawing close to God.

Joseph prospered knowing God. He became a rich ruler in Egypt, and in due time, was reunited with his family.

The Bible says, For the Lord thy God is a merciful God, he will not forsake thee . . . (Deuteronomy 4: 31).

Reading scripture, praying, and listening to God's word helps us know that God never abandons us.

Dear Lord, I thank you for being here with me when I call upon you. Forgive me if I have sinned, and bring me back into fellowship with family, friends, and believers. Amen.

Abandoned -- New Testament

And they all forsook him, and fled.
Mark 14: 50

Jesus was abandoned by his disciples when servants of the high priest came to arrest him for claiming to be the Son of God.

It was a desolate lonely experience for Jesus to be escorted to the palace of the high priest in the dark of the night, but he had already prayed about the matter.

Jesus maintained his integrity, and knowing God was with him, still claimed to be the Son of the Blessed in front of the high priest.

We should keep such faith, for God never abandons us (Hebrews 13: 5).

I felt abandoned one evening after my wife left me, but I awoke the next morning and went to a church service where someone in the hallway exclaimed, "God is here."

Well, God is here, and He often intercedes for us at desolate times (Romans 8: 26-27).

We don't know what to do or where to go, and yet God's merciful love descends from heaven to accompany and guide us.

And Jesus intercedes for us (Romans 8: 34; Hebrews 7: 24-25).

So when feeling abandoned by people, consider that God and Christ are here and never abandons us.

Dear Lord, I thank you for Christ Jesus who has died for my sin and intercedes for me. May I share this good news with other people who feel abandoned. Amen.

Adultery – Old Testament

And David sent messengers, and took her; and she came in unto him, and he lay with her; for she was purified from her uncleanness: and she returned unto her house.

2 Samuel 11: 4

King David was on the rooftop of his house when he saw Bathsheba washing herself, but he was also at the heights of sinful lust, because he subsequently had intimate relations with her.

(Bathsheba was married to Uriah, who was a soldier out fighting a losing battle for the king.)

Perhaps if David would have been with his men, they might have won that battle—and David would have won the battle over the lust of the flesh.

Sin always causes needless suffering: Uriah died in battle, the child David conceived with Bathsheba died, and David spent much of his time in remorsefulness after God sent Nathan the prophet to confront him about sin.

Consider reading Psalms 32 and 51 to see how David repented of sin and restored his faith in God.

God wants all of our attention on Him rather than a false idol, or an inordinate affair with another person.

"Thou shalt have no other gods before me" (Exodus 20: 3).

Dear Lord, Have mercy on me and forgive my sin. I humble myself from this sin of adultery. You are righteous and may this marriage be restored by mercy, forgiveness, and truth. Amen.

Adultery--New Testament

And he saith unto them, "Whosoever shall put away his wife, and marry another, committeth adultery against her. And if a woman shall put away a husband, and marry another, she committeth adultery."

Mark 10: 11-12

Divorcing a spouse commits adultery because a faithful commitment of togetherness has been made in front of a holy God who expects vows to be fulfilled.

But Jesus takes the issue of adultery further and says: "That whosoever looketh on a woman to lust after her hath committed adultery already in his heart" (Matthew 5: 28).

In other words, keep passionate desires only upon the person you've married.

But if adultery does occur, God has provided Jesus as a sacrifice for sin.

A woman, who was found in the act of adultery, was brought to Jesus for judgment, but Jesus did not condemn her (John 8: 1-14).

He instead received her and said, "Go, and sin no more".

Dear Father in Heaven, I come to you in humble confession and ask forgiveness for my adulterous act. Restore this marriage I pray. Amen.

Afraid – Old Testament

In God I will put my trust. I will not fear what man can do unto me.
Psalms 56:11

The psalmist David was in constant fear throughout his life battling a giant named Goliath, running from the jealousy of King Saul, and participating in wars against other nations, but he had the right attitude when fearful -- trust in God.

Consider also reading Psalms 27 to see how David faced fear and acknowledged God's presence: he strengthened himself in the Lord and sought God's leading.

The Lord is my light and my salvation; whom shall I fear? The Lord is the strength of my life; of whom shall I be afraid (Psalms 27: 1).

There are many things that make us afraid, but knowing God is in control will comfort us.

David had also sought shelter in God's temple, and he glorified the beauty of God.

For in the time of trouble he shall hide me in his pavilion; in the secret of his tabernacle shall he hide me; he shall set me up upon a rock (Psalms 27: 5).

And so we are encouraged: Wait (hope) on the Lord; be of good courage, and he shall strengthen thine heart. Wait (hope), I say, on the Lord (Psalms 27: 14).

Dear Lord, Your guidance and comfort is real, and I trust you to help me. May I be still and know that you are God. Amen.

Afraid – New Testament

"Peace I leave unto you, my peace I give unto you; not as the world giveth, give I unto you. Let not your heart be troubled, neither let it be afraid."
John 14: 27

Jesus is comforting his disciples with words of peace because soldiers will soon be coming to take him away to the high priest for crucifixion.

But Jesus still gives peace.

After Jesus died and arose from the grave, he appeared to his disciples to give them an eternal peace.

"Peace be unto you; as my Father hath sent me, even so send I you."

And when he had said this, he breathed on them, and saith unto them, "Receive ye the Holy Spirit" (John 20: 21-22).

Thank God for Jesus who allows us have the Comforter of the Holy Spirit regardless of what happens on earth (John 14: 26, 15: 26).

But aside from a personal peaceful relationship with Jesus, much of our fear comes from ungodly men who have weaponry in the skies, terrorists on the streets, and deceivers in the marketplace.

But we are not to fear man.

It is God whom we ultimately fear because he has power to cast the soul into heaven or hell (Luke 12: 5); therefore, we should obey his commandments and trust him for comfort and safety.

Dear Lord, I praise you for Jesus who takes away my sin, and I trust you to give me peace. May I find comfort in your holy place. Amen.

Aging – Old Testament

And Moses was an hundred and twenty years old when he died; his eye was not dim, nor his natural force abated.

Deuteronomy 34: 7

Moses was a man who looked good at his death -- but he had actively worked for God in his life.

He had taken care of his father-in-law's sheep, walked up and down a mountain to receive God's Ten Commandments, and led a group of people across the Red Sea through a wilderness to God's land of promise.

His people would also have been physically fit: to gather wood for fire, food to eat, materials for shelter, and articles to make clothing.

We should be so busy, but if we are sitting around and not doing anything: we are slowly aging.

One scripture gives us wisdom: By much slothfulness the building decayeth, and through idleness of the hands, the house droppeth through (Ecclesiastes 10: 18).

Our house may be deteriorating along with our body if we don't get up and work for God.

Be open to God's vision for your life, and then get busy to fulfill the call.

Dear Lord, I thank you for your presence here today. My body sometimes gets weak, but your spirit makes me alive. Amen.

Aging -- New Testament

And when he was gone forth into the way, there came one running, and kneeled to him, and asked him, "Good Master, what shall I do that I may inherit eternal life?"

Mark 10: 17

A rich man wanted to know how to live a long life, so Jesus quoted several of the Ten Commandments to which the man agreed -- but then Jesus told the man to go and sell what he had and give to the poor, and come, take up the cross and follow me (Mark 10: 17-22).

Jesus knew earthly possessions would be a burden to cause unnecessary worry and aging, whether they were carried around physically or spiritually: they sap the strength of a person.

We are to serve God in the Spirit, which gives us life.

Consider also reading Ephesians 4: 23-24 to be renewed in the spirit of the mind.

And that ye put on the new man, which after God, is created in righteousness and true holiness.

When we accept Christ as Savior, the old person is gone, and we become a new creature in Christ (2 Corinthians 5: 17).

Dear Father in Heaven, I thank you for eternal life through Christ Jesus who is able to renew me. Forgive my sins I pray through Christ and allow me to serve you in newness of spirit. Amen.

Alcohol – Old Testament

"... neither have ye drunk wine or strong drink: that ye might know that I am the Lord your God."
Deuteronomy 29: 6

God reminded the Israelites that they had no drink for pleasure in the wilderness and yet they were sustained.

God's spirit will sustain us in times of drought, poverty, or desolation.

The wisest thing we can do is make sure our relationship with the Lord is right, and then he will give us pleasure from the fruit of the vine.

Alcohol does have some healthy benefits, according to the Bible.

The Bible says, give strong drink unto him that is ready to perish, and wine unto those that are of heavy hearts (Proverbs 31: 6).

But we are warned not to abuse drinking: Wine is a mocker, strong drink is raging: and whosoever is deceived thereby is not wise (Proverbs 20: 1).

Dear Lord, I trust you to keep me in the right place around the right people. May my body be purged of alcohol so I can live healthy for your purpose. Amen.

Alcohol -- New Testament

"Verily I say unto you, I will drink no more of the fruit of the vine until that I drink it new in the kingdom of God."
Mark 14: 25

Jesus would not allow himself to drink for pleasure until he performed the will of his Father by dying for the people's sins.

That should be our attitude: first do the work of God by testifying, serving, and ministering, and then drink for pleasure at the end of the job.

Jesus was well aware of the benefits of a little alcohol when he made water into wine in Mark 2.

But some people abuse drinking alcohol and become addicted: their sorrow and troubles increase, and they wonder how to withdraw from alcohol addiction.

The world offers educational classes, a new pill, or even another fancy drink, but there is only one way to cure the addiction: accept Jesus Christ as Savior who has victory over the lust of the flesh (read Galatians 5:17-24).

The Bible says: That if thy shalt confess with thy mouth the Lord Jesus, and shalt believe in thine heart that God hath raised him from the dead, thou shalt be saved (Romans 10: 9).

Dear Lord, May I abstain from alcohol and learn more about your word which gives me life. Grant me a new life in Christ Jesus I pray. Amen.

Anger – Old Testament

And it came to pass, as soon as he came nigh unto the camp, that he saw the calf, and the dancing; and Moses anger waxed hot, and he cast the tables out of his hands, and brake them beneath the mount.

Exodus 32: 19

Moses got so angry at seeing the people dancing around a false idol that he threw down the stone tablets which had the Ten Commandments on them and they broke.

That only made matters worse because then he had to go back up the mountain to make two more tablets.

When we see things that make us angry such as false worship, violence, or abuse, turning to God helps us find peace and guidance.

The Bible gives us more advice, Cease from anger, and forsake wrath, fret not thyself in any wise to do evil (Psalms 37: 8).

But God does get angry: he is angry with the wicked everyday (Psalms 7: 11).

He had Moses divide the golden calf idolaters from those people who were on the Lord's side, and three thousand idolaters were slain.

May we love God enough to be on the right side of anger.

Dear Lord, I pray you take this anger away so that I can have peace. I look to you for the right and wise thing to do. Amen.

Anger -- New Testament

And they come to Jerusalem: and Jesus went into the temple, and began to cast out them that sold and bought in the temple, and overthrew the tables of the moneychangers, and the seats of them that sold doves.
Mark 11: 15

Jesus got so angry at seeing God's holy temple being made a marketplace for the buying and selling of sacrificial offerings that he chased out the moneychangers and animal sellers.

We may also get angry at seeing irreverent activity.

If our anger is justified, then we should try and work out a solution without committing violence.

But if our anger is unjustified, Jesus says we are in danger of judgment and we should make peace with our adversaries quickly (Matthew 5: 22-26).

Possibly the best advice comes from the Book of Ephesians: Be ye angry, and sin not; let not the sun go down upon your wrath (Ephesians 4: 26).

In other words, before the day ends, make peace with both God and man.

Dear Lord, It makes me upset to see unrighteousness, but you are the great Judge and I know you will fix this situation. Grant me the wisdom to know what to do. Amen.

Argument (Rebukement) – Old Testament

"Who am I that I should go unto Pharaoh, and that I should bring forth the children of Israel out of Egypt?"   Exodus 3: 11

Moses was constantly arguing with God about how to lead or discipline the people, but God won every time.

The prophet Isaiah said it best, "Woe unto him that striveth with his maker! . . . Shall the clay say to him that fashioneth it, 'What makest thou?' . . ." (Isaiah 45: 9).

The biblical patriarch Job also debated with God, and then was reproved boldly when God came to him out of a whirlwind; "Who is this that darkeneth counsel by words without knowledge" (Job 38-41).

But we will have disagreements with people: Proverbs 17: 17 says a brother is born for adversity.

Fortunately, God has established human relation policies, the court, and judges to determine appropriate resolutions (Exodus 21-23: 1-9).

And then there are times to confront a person about sin: we are not to allow sin to come upon a neighbor (Leviticus 19: 17).

But we should be wise to search out God's scriptures before correcting someone: it may be that we are the ones who need corrected.

In contrast to those proverbs, there are people that should not be rebuked: Answer not a fool according to his folly, lest thou also be like unto him (Proverbs 26: 4); and rebuke not a scorner, lest he hate thee (Proverbs 9: 8).

Dear Lord, May I refrain from debates and disputes, yet if I must argue, may I do so in the spirit of brotherhood, righteousness, and established rules. Amen.

Argument - New Testament

And the Pharisees said unto him, "Behold, why do they on the Sabbath day that which is not lawful? " And he said unto them, "Have ye never read what David did, when he had need, and was hungry, he, and they that were with him."

Mark 2: 24-25

Jesus is arguing for a new Sabbath day regulation of mercy.

But he also argued that he was the Son of God, an earthly temple would be destroyed, and he would rise from the grave.

Arguments take place daily in courtrooms, business offices, homes, and on playgrounds. These are good opportunities to mediate issues in the world but also proclaim the righteousness of God.

If we are committed to God, we will be arguing for godly principles knowing that expressing truth and mercy are part of God's will.

And the Bible advises us to rebuke liars and hypocrites sharply, that they may be sound in the faith (read Titus 1: 9--2: 15).

But the Apostle Paul says to do all things without murmurings and disputings that ye may be blameless and harmless, the sons of God without rebuke . . . (Philippians 2: 14-15).

Dear Lord, It upsets me to argue, but at times this has to be done. May I receive the strength and facts to argue righteously with you as witness. Amen.

Believe – Old Testament

And he believed in the Lord; and he counted it to him for righteousness.

Genesis 15: 6

Abraham believed in the Lord because he received several visions that came true: he inherited good land for farming, received a family, and found safety from enemies.

But there will be problems on the way to receiving such blessings.

For Abraham, a famine occurred and he had to travel to Egypt to find food. Then he had marriage problems with Sarah when his maid became pregnant with his child.

Satan will do anything to stop us from believing in God and receiving blessings but when God ordains something, it will come true.

The Bible says: "The Lord of hosts hath sworn, saying, surely as I have thought, so shall it come to pass, and as I have purposed, so shall it stand" (Isaiah. 14: 24).

Dear Lord, I believe you will perform that which you have shown me. May I be a faithful servant who carries out your mission for life. Amen.

Believe -- New Testament

And they said, "Believe on the Lord Jesus Christ, and thou shalt be saved, and thy house."
Acts 16: 31

This is what the men in the prison told the guard who had left the prison door open.

The guard was scared when he saw the door open. His discipline would have been severe for letting these men of faith escape.

The Apostle Paul also yelled out, "Do thyself no harm; for we are all here".

After the prison guard heard and saw the works of these men of faith, he too believed in Jesus, and the people in his house were saved.

Jesus says, "I am the resurrection, and the life; he that believeth in me, though he were dead, yet shall he live" (John 11: 25).

This is our faith.

There is no hope in the world, but with Jesus, there is hope to live life for God's glory and to live after death in the resurrection.

Jesus raised the lame, opened the eyes of the blind, loosened the tongues of the mute, and saved people from death.

Many people then saw the miracles Jesus performed and they believed (John 2: 23).

Dear God, I believe in the resurrection of Christ to take away my sins and give me salvation. Amen.

Building -- Old Testament

Make thee an ark of gopher wood; rooms shalt thou make in the ark, and shalt pitch it within and without with pitch.   **Genesis 6: 14**

God instructed Noah to build an ark because a catastrophic flood was coming to remove all the evil from the world.

The ark would be made out of gopher wood and be sealed with tar; and it would be 300 by 50 by 30 cubits, length, width, and height.

It would have rooms, doors, windows, and be three levels high to hold all of Noah's family and a lot of animals.

But when God builds things, he builds things just right.

The Bible says: Except the Lord build the house, they labor in vain that build it . . . (Psalms 127: 1).

The flood came and the ark rose above the earth for 150 days until the waters receded, and then the ark rested on land, and Noah removed the cover lid to see the dry land.

God will keep us protected when the shelter is built right, but more importantly, may our lives be built around God's word.

God designed His Word to give us a foundation for a good life.

Consider reading the Ten Commandments in the Book of Exodus 20: 1-17.

It's a good place to start building a foundation.

Dear Father in Heaven, May I build according to your plan and make a sure foundation for my life. Thank you for the Word of truth. Amen.

Building -- New Testament

"Therefore whosoever heareth these sayings of mine, and doeth them, I will liken him unto a wise man, who built his house on a rock." Matthew 7: 24

Building a house on a rock is wise because the foundation is stable.

The same is true with a man who builds his life around the sayings of Jesus.

"A new commandment I give unto you, that ye love one another; as I have loved you, that ye also love one another" (John 13: 34).

Loving one another keeps us in the right spirit to build relationships.

And then there's the reverent golden rule: "Therefore, all things whatever ye would that men should do to you, do ye even so to them; for this is the law and the prophets" (Matthew 7: 12).

But first, we should get to know Jesus personally by reading the Book of St. John, Chapters 14-17 and listening to his intimate prayers. "Let not your heart be troubled, ye believe in God, believe also in me" (John 14: 1).

Coming to this stricken Savior in sickness, persecution, injury, rape, emotional suffering, financial ruin, torture, or isolation, is the only remedy to build or re-build a life.

With Jesus in our lives, our feet walk with grace, our words speak of wisdom, and our actions show mercy, by belief.

Dear God, I praise you for being here and building my faith in Jesus. May I complete the work you show me and may I build using the right materials of faith and trust. Amen.

Children – Old Testament

"And ye shall teach them your children, speaking of them when thou sittest in thine house, and when thou walkest by the way, when thou liest down, and when thou riseth up."

Deuteronomy 11: 19

God wants us to tell all our children about the law, ordinances, love, and mercy of God.

We should also tell them the story about how the Hebrews were freed from slavery; with a mighty hand, and an outstretched arm; for He brought them out of bondage from serving a Egyptian Pharaoh (Deuteronomy 28: 6).

Teaching children to fear and respect God helps them live long lives and gives them confidence (Deuteronomy 11: 21).

But children will also need discipline.

The Bible says: Withhold not correction from a child . . . (Proverbs 23: 13).

The rod and reproof give wisdom, but a child left to himself bringeth his mother to shame (Proverbs 29: 15).

Children are a blessing when raised according to Godly principles.

Lo, children are a heritage from the Lord; and the fruit of the womb is his reward (Psalms 127: 3).

Dear Lord, Thank you for being here and helping me raise my children. Bless us as a family Lord, have mercy on us, and keep us together. Amen.

Children -- New Testament

And ye fathers, provoke not your children to wrath: but bring them up in the nurture and admonition of the Lord.
Ephesians 6: 4

Raising a child in the nurture and admonition of the Lord shows patience, wisdom, love, guidance, and mercy.

But children best learn by our own actions, because they usually imitate what we do.

So as parents, we should personally know God by confession of faith and its practice.

Then we can teach our children to pray, so they will know what to do in times of trouble, how to make prudent decisions, and how to live wisely.

Consider reading Bible stories, encouraging participation with other children, and get them involved in a church group.

Jesus, as a young child, was in the temple daily learning about God and gaining wisdom.

Jesus loved the little children: "Permit the little children to come unto me, and forbid them not; for of such is the kingdom of God" (Mark 10: 14).

Encourage your children, and provoke them not to anger.

.

Dear Lord, Keep us together in the love and mercy of Jesus, who died for our sins. I will encourage my child daily with your help. Amen.

Confession – Old Testament

When I kept silence, my bones waxed old through my roaring all the day long.
Psalms 32: 3

King David is talking about his pain of keeping silent about his sin with Bathsheba.

Our bones will become old and pain will exist if we don't confess sin.

The Bible says: He that covereth his sins shall not prosper, but whoso confesseth and forsaketh them shall have mercy (Proverbs 28: 13).

God wants us to confess sins so we can have mercy and life, and God is faithful to forgive our sins when we bow to Him in confession (2 Chronicles 7: 14).

Dear God, "Have mercy upon me, O God, according to Thy loving kindness: according unto the multitude of Thy tender mercies blot out my transgressions. Wash me thoroughly from mine iniquity, cleanse me from my sin. For I acknowledge my transgressions and my sin is ever before me" (Psalms 51: 1-3). Amen.

Confession -- New Testament

If we confess our sins, he is faithful and just to forgive us our sins, and to cleanse us from all unrighteousness.

1 John 1: 9

Before confession can take place, there must be an acknowledgment of the sin: an immoral action has occurred.

But rather than be severely punished, God in His mercy sent His Son Jesus to earth through the virgin mother Mary as a sinless man to be a perfect sacrifice for our sin.

How great this is to know we can be freed of sin by belief in the sacrificial death of the Christ and his resurrection into the heavens above!

But it takes remorsefulness, humbleness, and sorrow.

Consider humility and prayer to God when sin begins to overflow in your life.

Jesus says, "Whosoever shall not receive the kingdom of God as a little child, he shall not enter into it" (Mark 10: 15).

Jesus also said to go to the Father in secret and pray -- and He will reward you openly (Matthew 6: 6).

Dear God, I bow down before you in humble confession. Please forgive me. I acknowledge my transgression and commit myself to your righteous ways. Thank you for Jesus who died for my sin. Amen.

Confidence – Old Testament

"Have not I commanded thee? Be strong and of good courage; be not afraid, neither be thou dismayed; for the Lord thy God is with thee wherever thou goest."
Joshua 1: 9

These are the words from God to Joshua before leading the people to the land of promise.

But Joshua had known God since he was young man: he had worshipped him in the tabernacle and saw him in a cloudy pillar (Exodus 33: 11).

Confidence comes from God. But if we don't know God, we have no true confidence.

The Bible says: In the fear of the Lord is strong confidence, and his children shall have a place of refuge (Proverbs 14: 26).

But if sin is in our lives, we do not have God's confidence. If anything, we have His condemnation.

In an earlier battle, the Israelites were defeated by the Amalekites and the Canaanites because of sin.

Moses had told the people, "Go not up, for the Lord is not among you; that ye be not smitten before your enemies" (Numbers 14: 42). And the Israelites had also been murmuring against God (Numbers 14: 27).

Following Joshua, who had God's confidence, the Israelites crossed the Jordan River and entered their land of promise.

Dear Lord, You are my confidence. I put you first in my life to achieve great things for your glory. Amen.

Confidence -- New Testament

Jesus answered and said unto him, "If a man love me, he will keep my words; and my Father will love him, and we will come in unto him, and make our abode with him."

John 14: 23

Having Jesus and God in our lives gives us great confidence, because Jesus is the propitiation for sins and God grants us forgiveness (1 John 2: 1-2).

And then the Holy Spirit intercedes for us according to the will of God (Romans 8: 26).

This is great confidence to have the trinity of God's parsonage with us.

But if we don't know Jesus, Jesus says we are like the branches without a vine as described in John 15: 4: we can bear no fruit.

And so we are encouraged, "I am the vine, ye are the branches. He that abideth in me and I in him, the same bringeth forth much fruit, for without me, you can do nothing" (John 15: 5).

It is the spirit of life in Christ Jesus that gives us confidence (Romans 8: 10).

God shows us what to do, where to go, how to get there, and how to get things done before it all takes place, and we know that what God purposes will come true.

We also know that he hears us, and whatever we ask, we know that we have the petitions we desired of him (1 John 5: 15).

Dear Lord, Thank you for giving me confidence through Christ Jesus. I can do all things through Christ who strengthens me. Amen.

Confusion – Old Testament

The proud have had me greatly in derision, yet have I not declined from thy law.
Psalms 119: 51

Satan's desire is to keep a person constantly confused, but knowing God's law rejects moral confusion, for His statutes are right.

But many of us don't know God's law, which may cause us to flee seven ways before enemies, be consumed with madness, and have sorrow of mind (read Deuteronomy 28: 15-68).

Consider humbling yourself when confused and remember that God is always in control. Read the scriptures and pray earnestly for God's truth.

The Bible says, Thou shalt keep, therefore, his statutes, and his commandments, which I command thee this day, that it may go well with thee (Deuteronomy 4: 40).

The simplicity of life's requirement might be summed up by Micah 6: 8: He hath shown thee, O man, what is good; and what doth the Lord require of thee, but to do justly, and to love mercy, and to walk humbly with thy God?

Dear Father in Heaven, I thank you for your truth and a stable mind, and knowing right from wrong. May I humble myself under your great hand so that I have peace. Amen.

Confusion -- New Testament

Wherefore, it is also contained in the scriptures, "Behold, I lay in Zion a chief corner stone, elect, precious: and he that believeth on him shall not be confounded."
1 Peter 4: 6

Belief in Jesus eliminates religious confusion because he is a total sacrifice for sins (Hebrews 10: 1-14).

Jesus eliminates worldly confusion because he proved the devil was a liar from the beginning (John 8: 12-59).

And he eliminates moral confusion because he intercedes for us and gives us examples of how to love one another.

Upon acceptance of Jesus, we become a righteous people who know the truth.

The scriptures also help us discern who is of God and who is a deceiver: Beloved, believe not every spirit, but test the spirits whether they are of God (1 John 4: 1).

The great teacher Nicodemus was confused, so in the darkness of his life he came to Jesus.

And Jesus said, "Verily, verily, I say unto thee: 'We speak that which we do know, and testify to that which we have seen; and ye receive not our witness' " (John 3: 11).

Jesus gives us some more good advice, "But let your communication be, Yea, yea; Nay, nay; for whatever is more than these cometh of evil" (Matthew 5: 37).

We are not to be immature, tossed to and fro, and carried about with every wind of doctrine . . . but, speak the truth in love (Ephesians 4: 14-15).

Dear Father in Heaven, I put my trust in you to reject confusion and rest in the truth. Amen.

Courage – Old Testament

And David said to Saul, 'Let no man's heart fail because of him; thy servant will go and fight with this Philistine."

1 Samuel 17: 32

One of the most courageous acts in the Old Testament is when the young boy David went to battle against a giant named Goliath and killed him.

But David did not go alone: God was with him.

When there are giants in our lives, we should also invoke God's name for courage.

Neither did David go without experience: for he had previously killed a lion and a bear with God's help.

Though Goliath was armored with a helmet, breastplate, leg ware, and a javelin with a spearhead, David had only a slingshot, some stones, and the Lord.

As David invoked the name of God, he slung a stone at Goliath's forehead and Goliath went down.

The Bible says, Through God we shall do valiantly; for he it is who shall tread down our enemies (Psalms 60: 12).

God is a partner we can count trust to defeat the enemy, but we must call on him before the battle.

Dear Lord, With you, all things are indeed possible. Strengthen me to be courageous for your sake. Amen.

Courage -- New Testament

But Peter and John answered and said unto them, "Whether it is right in the sight of God to hearken unto you more than unto God, judge ye".
Acts 4: 19

The Apostles were courageously talking back to the Sanhedrin council despite being threatened with jail and beatings for preaching Christ as Savior.

Testifying about Christ has it dangers, and Jesus confirms this when he says, "If they have persecuted me, they will also persecute you" (John 15: 20).

The Apostles did not faint when threatened but turned to God in prayer, "And now, Lord, behold their threatenings; and grant unto thy servants, that with all boldness they may speak thy word" (Acts 4: 29).

When faced with fear and needing courage, consider calling on God for help.

Each of us who believes in Christ sacrifices a life of personal desire to fulfill God's desire, and there will be dangerous circumstances.

The Apostle Paul has inspired us and said, "I can do all things through Christ who strengtheneth me" (Philippians 4: 13).

Dear Lord, Your presence here encourages me, and I thank you in advance for protecting me and yet witnessing for your glory. Have mercy on me I pray. Amen.

Crying – Old Testament

And she sat apart from him, and lifted up her voice, and wept.
Genesis 21: 16

Hagar's child was out of water to drink, so Hagar set the child off a good distance in the wilderness so she wouldn't see the child's death.

But God came along and saw Hagar's grief and showed her a well of water for the child.

God said, "Fear not; for God hath heard the voice of the lad where he is. Arise, lift up the lad, and hold him in thine hand; for I will make him a great nation."

Hagar went to the well and filled the skin with water and gave the lad drink (Genesis 17-19).

God knew the sad condition of Hagar and the child, and He knows our situation.

The Bible says: God is nigh unto those who are of a broken heart, and saveth such as be of a contrite spirit (Psalms 34: 18).

Our tears may flow with grief but God is still here for comfort and guidance.

Dear Father in Heaven, I thank you for being close to me in my tears. Comfort me and restore my strength I pray. Amen.

Crying -- New Testament

Jesus wept.

John 11: 35

Jesus cried because his friend Lazarus has died, and he wasn't in the area at the time of his sickness.

But Jesus didn't sorrow for long; he went to the tomb where Lazarus was laid to rest and performed a miracle.

And when he thus had spoken, he cried with a loud voice, "Lazarus, come forth" (John 11: 43).

And Lazarus came forth.

We should gather strength in the time of a death to perform a good deed and give God the glory.

The Bible says the lamb Jesus is in the midst of the throne . . . and shall lead them to fountains of living waters: and God shall wipe away all tears from their eyes (Revelation 7: 17).

Blessed are they that mourn, for they shall be comforted (Matthew 5: 4).

Dear Father in Heaven, I thank you for being here amidst my tears, and I praise you for Jesus who gives me the strength to live for you. Amen.

Death – Old Testament

And it came to pass after these things, Joshua, the son of Nun, the servant of the Lord, died, being one hundred and ten years old.
Joshua 24: 29

Joshua died at a good old age but before he passed away he testified of God's saving presence in front of the leaders of Israel and recollected the events of the past that had led to the people's freedom (Joshua 24: 1-13).

That's what we want to at the end of life – testify of God's saving presence and works during life.

But if we have differences with God, now is the time for acknowledging them and asking forgiveness.

For in death there is no remembrance of thee; in the grave who shall give thee thanks (Psalms 6: 5).

Being forgiven by God allows us to freely testify in life – and to be at peace upon death.

Dear Heavenly Father, I thank you for life, and I testify of your saving presence. Grant me mercy, peace, and rest, I pray. Amen.

Death -- New Testament

"For God so loved the world, that he gave his only begotten Son, that whosoever believeth in Him should not perish, but have everlasting life."

John 3: 16

Jesus overcame death by his resurrection from the grave but many people had trouble believing.

The Apostle Thomas wanted to see the nail prints and the blood in Christ's body: when he saw, he believed (John 20: 25-29).

God forbid we need to see wounds and blood before we believe in the risen Christ at death.

When the shadows becomes longer and the vision blurs, the body moves slower and the sounds soften, God's Holy Spirit increases to give us comfort and peace.

Jesus says, "I am the resurrection and the life: he that believeth in me, though he were dead, yet shall he live. And whosoever liveth and believeth in me shall never die. Believest thou this?" (John 11: 25-26).

The choice is ours. Resting in the arms of a loving Savior for an eternity is worth bowing before Him in life by confession of faith.

Dear Lord, I praise you for sending Jesus to free me from the pains of death and give me peace. I believe in the Holy Ghost, the forgiveness of sins, and life everlasting. Amen.

Debt – Old Testament

"... Thy servant my husband is dead; and thou knowest that thy servant did fear the Lord: and the creditor is come to take my two sons to be bondmen."

2 Kings 4: 1

A woman was about to lose her two children because of money being owed, so she looked to the man of God Elisha for some wisdom.

Elisha told her to go home and divide what little oil she had and put it in separate containers to sell and pay off the debt.

Wisdom may suggest we divide what little we have and make it last longer or sell something to pay off a debt.

But the only real debt we should have is praising God every day and witnessing for Him.

Psalms 23 tells us to trust the Lord for our needs: The Lord is my shepherd, I shall not want [lack] (Psalms 23: 1).

If we have borrowed a tangible asset, we should work on paying it back.

We don't want to be known as wicked people described in Psalms 37: 21: the wicked borroweth, and payeth not again; but the righteous showeth mercy, and giveth.

Possibly the writer of Ecclesiastes gives us the best advice: Better is it that thou shouldest not vow, than to vow and not pay (Ecclesiastes 5: 5).

Dear Father in Heaven, Please show me the way to repay this debt. May I never borrow again. I trust you to supply my needs. Amen.

Debt -- New Testament

"The servant, therefore, fell down, and worshiped him, saying, 'Lord, have patience with me, and I will pay thee all."
Matthew 18: 26

Jesus tells a parable about a poor servant owing money to his master and the master requiring payment. The poor servant bowed down before his master and was granted forgiveness.

But the same poor servant had a man who owed him money – and he would not forgive.

So the servant's lord got angry with him and sent interrogators, saying the servant had been forgiven yet would not forgive his worker.

That servant would be sent to his creditors' tormentors – and would have to work to pay off his debt.

Mercy should be the priority when a debt is owed or in demand. Nevertheless, if money is owed, it should be paid to fulfill the promise.

Christ's prayer helps guide us, "And forgive us our debts, as we forgive our debtors" (Matthew 6: 12).

But if we are in debt to sin, Christ's death on the cross has paid the price.

Upon confession and redemption of sin, we are free to serve and worship the living God (Romans 3: 24-26; 1 Peter 1: 18-19).

Dear Lord, I ask for patience paying off this debt and I promise never to get in monetary debt again. I am reminded to witness for you about the freedom Jesus gives by his sacrifice for sin. Amen.

Devil – Old Testament

Now the Serpent was more subtle than any beast of the field which the Lord God had made. And he said unto the woman, "Yea, hath God said, Ye shall not eat of every tree of the garden?"

Genesis 3: 1

This is the first time the devil serpent is mentioned in the Bible as the first woman Eve is offered an opportunity to eat from the tree of knowledge of good and evil in disobedience to God's command. The woman ate, her husband ate, and they were both chastised by God, who also disciplined the devil.

If you submit to the devil, there will be the consequences of discipline and punishment from God, who loves us enough to keep us on the right path for blessings.

God issued these decrees: Eve's desire would be to her husband and bear children in sorrow; Adam was to work by the sweat of his face; and the devil was cursed to crawl on his belly.

The Biblical man Job also faced the devil: Now there was a day when the Sons of God came to present themselves before the Lord, and Satan came also among them (Job 1: 6).

Job lost all he had including his health. Yet Job held onto his faith in the living God to restore his life.

When Satan comes around, stay around God's throne for victory, but it may mean to repent in ashes and dust like Job.

Dear Father in Heaven, Thank you for having power over the devil. When Satan comes around, I need your strength to help me. Protect me and have mercy I pray. Amen.

Devil -- New Testament

Be sober, be vigilant; because your adversary the devil, as a roaring lion, walketh about, seeking whom he may devour: whom resist steadfast in the faith, knowing that the same afflictions are accomplished in our brethren that are in the world.
1 Peter 5: 8-9

Peter advises us to be on guard against the devil.

But we must know the description of the devil.

The Bible lists these traits: he lies, cheats, steals, murders, deceives, presumes, and is full of pride, malignant, envious, and covetous (greedy); he has also been described as a serpent, wolf, and an angel of light.

Fortunately, Christ has defeated the devil because the devil has nothing in Christ (John 14: 30). Christ was sinless.

And when tempted by the devil in the wilderness, Christ quoted God's word and said God could not be tempted -- but to go away and worship God (Mark 4).

If the devil is in us, then we are advised to be humble, pray, and cease from eating food, as Jesus mentioned in freeing a possessed child from a demon (Mark 9: 29).

The writer James gives us some good advice: Submit yourselves, therefore, to God. Resist the devil, and he will flee from you (James 4: 7).

Dear Lord, I confront the devil in the power of Jesus Christ and your righteousness. but I am also humble enough to let you drive him away. Amen.

Disability – Old Testament

And as he passed over Penuel the sun rose upon him, and he halted upon his thigh.
Genesis 32: 31

Jacob became disabled when he failed to bless God and an angel knocked his thigh out of joint.

We may become disabled from failing to bless God; or possibly we are disabled from birth or have suffered a tragic accident. But if we know God, we are whole in the spirit.

We can glorify God in many ways: communicating, performing good works, or using what bodily members we have to inspire other people.

The Bible says God formed Jacob for His purpose -- to give Him glory (Isaiah 43: 1-13).

And God has formed us for His purpose.

Jacob was made whole in his faith after the visit by God's angel, and he visited his estranged brother Esau with blessings.

Dear Lord, I am complete with you, fully able to pray and serve. Have mercy upon me and may you be glorified in all that I do. Amen.

Disability -- New Testament

> . . . there was given to me a thorn in the flesh, the messenger of Satan to buffet me, lest I should be exalted above measure.
>
> 2 Corinthians 12: 7

The Apostle Paul took pleasure in his infirmity knowing it kept him humble and close to God.

Being disabled keeps us humble because we move slower and have pain as a reminder of the weakness of the flesh.

But in another biblical account of disability, a man was not only disabled but people were pushing him away so they could get in healing waters.

And then Jesus came along, and said, "Arise, take up thy bed, and walk" (John 5: 1-9). And the man arose and was healed.

Jesus cares. He knows, because he was defamed, persecuted, and laughed at; so he understands our disabilities.

Sick, disabled, and impotent people came to Jesus and received power from God (Matthew 15: 30).

Disabled in the world but able in God to do exceedingly above all we think or ask when we yield our members to Him (Ephesians 3:14-21).

God gives us the spirit of grace through Jesus to bear our infirmities (2 Corinthians 12: 9). And Jesus intercedes for our suffering (Hebrews 4: 14-16).

Dear Heavenly Father, Everyday is difficult in this body, but every day is precious because you fill me with the whole spirit. May I use my body to produce good work and testify of your name. Amen.

Discouragement – Old Testament

... And he requested for himself that he might die, and said, "It is enough!"   1 Kings 19: 4

Elijah was going through a rough time having escaped from the prophet killer Jezebel and now finding himself in the hot desert starving.

So he sat under a juniper tree hoping to die.

That's how we feel sometimes: wanting to die because things are going so bad.

But God sent an angel to touch Elijah.

Maybe Elijah was so beat up, tired, and distraught it took some physical contact to get his attention.

But then the angel said to get up, eat, and continue on the journey.

In the heat of the day, under the shade of the Almighty, we might hear the words that give us new life: "Arise, eat, and continue on the journey".

Consider some Proverbs which give us encouragement when there are dark times.

Hope deferred maketh the heart sick; but when the desire cometh, it is a tree of life (Proverbs 13: 12).

So we need patience to see hope come true, and we might ask ourselves what can make the situation better.

A merry heart maketh a cheerful countenance, but by sorrow of the heart, the spirit is broken (Proverbs 15: 13). So it's important to stay in a good emotional state of mind and consider what would bring happiness.

Dear Lord, I am discouraged by the events happening around me, but I am encouraged by your presence. Let me be faithful to achieve that which you want me to do. Amen.

Discouragement -- New Testament

And saith unto them, "My soul is exceeding sorrowful unto death: tarry ye here, and watch."
Mark 14: 34

Jesus was discouraged because the time was drawing near for him to die for the people's sins, but then he found his disciples sleeping at a time when soldiers would soon be coming to arrest him.

But he looked to God for encouragement as he walked off a short distance and began to pray.

That's what we need to do when discouraged; go to God in prayer.

It is easy to become so discouraged in a world of poverty, sickness, war, and tragedy, but God is still here in the spirit for encouragement.

He gave Jesus the strength to complete his calling, and he gives us strength to achieve great things for his name's sake.

We are also encouraged to exhort one another, as we see the day approaching (Hebrews 10: 25).

Consider the inspiration from Christ when a grieving father brought his son to Jesus for healing: "If thou canst believe, all things are possible to him that believeth" (Mark 9: 23).

Now the God of hope fill you with all joy and peace in believing, that ye may abound in hope through the power of the Holy Spirit (Romans 15: 13).

Dear Lord, Life can be so discouraging, but with you as the motivator through Christ Jesus, I am inspired to be courageous. Amen.

Divorce – Old Testament

> ... then let him write her a bill of divorcement, and give it in her hand, and send her out of his house.
> **Deuteronomy 24: 1**

Divorce was permitted in the Old Testament when the man felt his wife was unfavorable towards him, but he had the power to void or accept her words and actions during the marriage (Genesis 3: 16; Numbers 30: 6-8).

From the beginning, divorce was not meant to be; the man and woman were created in God's image to be together and multiply on the face of the earth (Genesis 1: 17).

They were given decrees, straight from the marriage maker: the woman was brought to the man for his suffering side to be a helper, and he was to cleave unto her.

Adam and Eve had some problems with the devil but they stayed together after God disciplined them, and they had a family.

Before getting divorced, make sure your relationship with God is intact: it may be you are getting divorced from God.

The Lord our God is one Lord (Deuteronomy 6: 4).

Dear Lord, You are the one I should truly be married to but I also pray for my spouse to come to know your love, mercy, and fellowship. Amen.

Divorce -- New Testament

But if the unbelieving depart, let him depart. A brother or a sister is not under bondage in such cases; but God hath called us unto peace.
1 Corinthians 7: 15

The Apostle Paul tries to justify the separation of an unbelieving spouse by saying there should be peace without bondage.

But marriage is a bond -- and Christ Jesus says a spouse should not divorce but in the case of fornication (Matthew 5: 32).

Jesus further says, "What therefore God hath joined together, let man not put asunder" (Matthew 19: 6).

When problems do occur within a marriage, scripture encourages mates to be kind to one another, tenderhearted, forgiving one another, even as God, for Christ's sake, hath forgiven you (Ephesians 4: 32).

Pray for a separated mate to find Jesus.

Regardless of what happens in a domestic marriage, Jesus is a mate for life.

Wherefore, my brethren, ye also are become dead to the law by the body of Christ; that ye should be married to another, even to him who is raised from the dead, that we should bring forth fruit unto God (Romans 7: 4).

Dear Lord, If I have sinned, forgive me of sin to be reconciled with you. I love you Lord, and I hope my mate loves you and finds your mercy. Amen.

Drugs – Old Testament

"Thou shalt not bow down thyself to them nor serve them; for I, the Lord thy God, am a jealous God . . ."

Exodus 20: 5

God will not take second place to drugs because he is a jealous God that wants to give us mercy, peace, and life.

To quit drugs, consider reading the Book of Isaiah Chapters 56-58 to learn about how separation to God brings blessings.

Replace drugs with good food, work, exercise, and faith in God.

God is more stable than any drug, and the side effects are holiness, righteousness, prosperity, and salvation.

And then there are the benefits of having good friends you can depend on and get respect from other people.

Your "drug friends" may mock you for awhile, but when you start to achieve good grades in school, perform good work projects, develop good friends, and make righteous earnings, you will get respect.

In another reading, a psalmist said he called on the name of the Lord and was saved from death; he was brought low -- but the Lord helped him ((Psalm 116: 4-8).

Dear Father in Heaven, you are the way for life and I commit my ways to you. I confess my inadequacies and solely trust you to provide me peace, happiness, and the work I need for a prosperous life. Amen.

Drugs – New Testament

And they that are Christ's have crucified the flesh with the affections and lust.
                                                    Galatians 5: 24

Christ Jesus gives us power over the temptation to take drugs because he has crucified the lusts of the flesh.

When a temptation comes to take a drug, look to Christ who sits on the right hand side of God for intervention and help (Hebrews 1: 3).

Read the scriptures, such as Galatians 5 which helps you understand just what the lust of the flesh is and how you can deny it with Christ.

Fasting, humility, and lowliness are attributes that destroy the drug addiction.

And claim a scripture to live by such as 1 Corinthians 3: 16-17: Know ye not that ye are the temple of God, and that the Spirit of God dwelleth in you? If any man defile the temple of God, him shall God destroy; for the temple of God is holy, which temple ye are.

Our bodies are to be used for God's purpose and service (1 Corinthians 6: 20; Romans 12).

God is faithful, who will not suffer you to be tempted above that ye are able, but will, with the temptation, also make a way to escape, that ye may be able to bear it (1 Corinthians 10: 13).

Dear Lord, I confess my sin and call on your name for help. Have mercy on me and renew me in the right spirit to love Jesus in body, mind, and soul. I can do all things though Christ who strengthens me. Amen.

Eating – Old Testament

And he humbled thee, and suffered thee to hunger, and fed thee with manna, which thou knewest not, that he might make thee know that man doth not live by bread only, but by every word that proceedeth out of the mouth of the Lord doth man live.
                                   Deuteronomy 8: 3

The Israelites suffered times of famine in the wilderness without any food but God sustained them with His spirit.

In times of famine, we might also consider God as provider, and consider advice from the psalmist: Trust in the Lord, and do good; so shalt thou dwell in the land, and verily thou shalt be fed (Psalms 37: 3).

Dietary regulations are found in the 11th Chapter of Leviticus; other than the commandment to eat from every tree of the garden except the tree of knowledge of good and evil.

A gift from God is to be able to eat, but we are expected to perform good works and acknowledge His presence

The Bible says: And also, that every man should eat and drink, and enjoy the good of all his labor, it the gift of God (Ecclesiastes 3: 13).

The words of Agur in the Book of Proverbs gives us some good advice: Remove far from me vanity and lies; give me neither poverty nor riches; feed me with food convenient for me (Proverbs 30: 8).

Dear Father in Heaven, I thank you for bread from earth but also your provision from heaven. Your Word feeds me wisdom so I can work and testify of your saving presence. Amen.

Eating -- New Testament

Hast thou faith? Have it to thyself before God. Happy is he that condemneth not himself in that thing which he alloweth.
Romans 14: 22

The rules for eating in the New Testament are in 14th chapter of Romans.

They basically state that eating something that strengthens faith in God is good, but eating something that causes a person to stumble or make mistakes is not good; therefore, God should be consulted in prayer before eating.

Consider personal prayer before each meal to make sure the food is agreeable with God.

However, the Bible also says the kingdom of God is not meat and drink but righteousness, peace, and joy in the Holy Ghost (Romans 14: 17).

In other words, we are to focus on what God wants us to do in the spirit of life and He will feed us our daily bread.

Jesus said not to worry about food for the body: the birds of the air neither sow, nor reap, nor gather into barns, but the Lord feeds them (Matthew 6: 28).

Dear Heavenly Father, I praise you for showing me what food is acceptable for my body, but also for Jesus who fills me with heavenly bread that gives me life everlasting. Amen.

Enemies -- Old Testament

And Saul cast the javelin; for he said, "I will smite David even to the wall with it." And David escaped from his presence twice.

1 Samuel 18: 11

King Saul considered David an enemy after David killed the giant Goliath in battle and gained fame among the people.

We may have enemies because someone becomes jealous or resentful, but that's a good time for turning to God in prayer.

David prayed for God to have judgment over Saul's actions, and Saul eventually died in battle.

That's what happens sometimes: the aggressive actions of a jealous person like Saul comes back upon him.

God is a great judge and avenger of innocent and humble people.

In fact, God becomes an enemy to our enemies when we love him and are obedient (Numbers 23: 22-33).

And God will have vengeance on His adversaries (Deuteronomy 32: 35).

We are encouraged by the proverb: When a man's ways please the Lord, he maketh even his enemies to be at peace with him (Proverbs 16: 7).

Dear Heavenly Father, Please spare me from this enemy's anger and take him away from me. Confront this enemy in righteousness and judgment as I keep you first in my life. Amen.

Enemies -- New Testament

And the Pharisees went forth and straightway took counsel with the Herodians against him, how they might destroy him.
Mark 3: 6

Jesus became an enemy of the Pharisees when he started healing on the Sabbath Day of rest.

Scribes and priests also considered Jesus an enemy because he was teaching a new doctrine (Luke 19: 47).

And the Jews tried to kill Jesus for claiming to be the Son of God (John 5: 18).

Jesus had lots of enemies just for proclaiming God's word.

And we will also have enemies for performing faith works.

When enemies present themselves, Jesus says to bless your enemies and pray for them who despitefully use you (Matthew 5: 43-44).

Such an attitude keeps us on the right path to perform God's will.

Giving an enemy over to God in prayer allows us to go and fulfill the great commission of spreading the gospel and salvation to every person on earth.

Dear Heavenly Father, I thank you for intercession to help me understand the enemy. May my enemy come to know the peace that comes through the precious blood of Jesus who died for us. Amen.

Evil – Old Testament

But it shall to come to pass, if thou wilt not hearken unto the voice of the Lord thy God, to observe to do all his commandments and his statutes which I command thee this day, that all these curses shall come upon thee, and overtake thee.	Deuteronomy 28: 15

The curses from God are listed in the 28th Chapter of Deuteronomy, and they are something no man wants part of: destruction, pestilence, fever, burning, madness, and slavery.

Consider the disobedience of Jonah, who failed to go to the town of Nineveh and preach judgment: he was cursed for being disobedient and found himself on a boat, only to be thrown overboard by the crewmen and swallowed by a big fish and spit upon a beach.

And then there's Cain, who killed his brother Abel and had to run for the rest of his life.

And Jacob, who lied to get his father's blessing and also had to run all over the country in fear of his brother.

The good news is God has power over all these evils. We need to only get right with God to be spared of them. The fear of the Lord is to hate evil (Proverbs 8: 13).

And we are advised to depart from evil and do good (Psalm 37: 27; Proverbs 3: 7).

Innumerable evils encompassed a psalmist -- iniquities consumed and shamed him -- but he made the Lord his trust for mercy and salvation (Psalm 40).

Dear Lord, Thank you for having control over evil. Your righteousness will prevail in this situation and I trust you to keep me safe. Amen.

Evil – New Testament

Let him eschew evil, and do good, let him seek peace, and ensue it.   **1 Peter 3: 11**

Before we can eschew evil, we must define it.

Adjectives for evil in the New Testament are slander, pride, deceit, maliciousness, backbiting, hatred, drunkenness, jealousy, malignity, covetousness, lust, self-willingness, idolatry, witchcraft, reveling, debate, false accusation, fierceness, and murder.

Meddling with any of those traits is meddling with evil.

But thankfully the risen Christ has conquered evil.

Mary, called Magdalene, was healed from seven demons by Christ (Luke 8: 2).

Jesus says evil comes from within the heart of man (Mark 7: 21-23). And this is why we should humble ourselves and turn to God in prayer; God can remove evil.

The Apostle Paul encourages us to abhor that which is evil (Romans 12: 9). Yet Jesus says in Matthew 5: 39 not to resist evil if someone has afflicted us or threatened a lawsuit.

Jesus prayed that we be delivered from the evil one (Luke 11: 4). But the Apostle Paul says to overcome evil with good (Romans 12: 21).

For the eyes of the Lord are over the righteous, and his ears are open unto their prayers; but the face of the Lord is against them that do evil (1 Peter 3: 12).

Dear Lord, I thank you for Jesus Christ who overcomes evil. And I invite him into my heart for protection, wisdom, and salvation. Amen.

Faith -- Old Testament

And Joshua blessed him, and gave unto Caleb, the son of Jephunneh, Hebron, for an inheritance.
Joshua 14: 13

Caleb received a portion of land he had spied out forty-five years earlier.

Being faithful does not have any time limits, as God is in charge of the benefits and extends blessings when he wants.

And faith does not always procure some material good -- but is more likely to give God glory in a matter, like God using Caleb as a man of war to defeat enemies.

But without faith, we can not please God, and in fact, we will be harshly judged.

People who sought their own desire rather than God's desire were confronted by their sin.

The Bible says, while their food was yet within their mouths, the wrath of God came upon them, and slew the fattest of them, and smote down the chosen men of Israel (Psalms 78: 30-31).

Faith to perform Godly works does not come without sacrifices or troubles. Caleb was slandered and threatened with stoning for reporting the land and its inhabitants could be seized.

And we will also have troubles before receiving God's promises. But if God has ordained something, it will come true, and just as important, is that we have peace for doing God's will.

The Bible says God's faithfulness does not fail (Psalms 89: 33).

Dear Lord, May I find the wonderful mission that you have for me and follow through by faith. Amen.

Faith – New Testament

Now faith is the substance of things hoped for, the evidence of things not seen. For by it, the elders received a good report.　　　　　　　　　　Hebrews 11: 1

Faith sees something in the future procured either as an asset or spiritual attribute but here in the 11th Chapter of Hebrews, practitioners of faith never received the promise: God having provided some better thing for us, that they without us should not be made perfect (Hebrews 11: 40). In other words, Jesus hadn't come along yet to complete the faith journey.

The greatest faith anyone can have is to believe in the risen Christ who gives salvation from sin. For he hath made him, who knew no sin, to be sin for us, that we might be made the righteousness of God in him (2 Corinthians 5: 21).

And then we want to produce good works by faith through Jesus: "Verily, verily, I say unto you, he that believeth on me, the works that I do shall he do also; and greater works than these shall he do, because I go unto my Father" (John 14: 12).

Christ incorporated faith works into his life by healing people, teaching them God's word for life, and fellowshipping with poor, destitute, and foreign people.

We should be so faithful -- and testify of the living God.

Dear Lord, Let me be faithful to complete the task you have shown me for life, but more so, may I know Jesus as my Savior. Amen.

Fellowship – Old Testament

And Moses and Aaron went and gathered together all the elders of the children of Israel; and Aaron spoke all the words which the Lord had spoken unto Moses, and did the signs of the sight of the people.
Exodus 4: 29-30

Fellowshipping with other believers can make great things happen such as when Moses, Aaron, and the elders of Israel got together and made a plan to free their people from slavery.

But first, fellowship should take place with God alone. The Bible says, Thou shalt love the Lord thy God with all thy heart, and with all thy soul, and with all they might (Deuteronomy 6: 5).

And then there are commandments to love people: Thou shalt not avenge, nor bear any grudge against the children of thy people; but thou shalt love thy neighbor as thyself: I am the Lord (Leviticus 19: 18).

Strangers are also to be loved: thou shalt love him as thyself (Leviticus 19: 34).

And in the congregation of believers, God wants glory for it all.

God has said, "I will be sanctified in them that come nigh me, and before all the people I will be glorified" (Leviticus 10: 3).

Dear Father in Heaven, I praise you for brothers and sisters but also for everyone in the world to come to know and worship you. Amen.

Fellowship – New Testament

> And when the scribes and Pharisees saw him eat with tax collectors and sinners, they said unto his disciples, "How is it that he eateth and drinketh with tax collectors and sinners?"
>
> Mark 2: 16

Jesus sets a wonderful example of fellowshipping when he sat down to eat with publicans, sinners, and the sick. He knew they needed to be fed God's word, so he humbly intermingled with them.

We should be so humble – not only talking with sinners but with people of different faiths and experiences. We share our lives and give testimony and faith in God. And we might find that we have something in common.

But we are warned by the Apostle Paul: Be ye not unequally yoked together with unbelievers; for what fellowship hath righteousness with unrighteousness? And what communion hath light with darkness? (2 Corinthians 6: 14).

Remember, we were once strangers to God (Ephesians 2: 19), but God had mercy to fellowship with us.

The Bible also encourages us to fellowship in the congregation of believers: Not forsaking the assembly of ourselves together, as the manner of some is; but exhorting one another: and so much the more, as ye see the day approaching (Hebrews 10: 25).

Dear Lord, I thank you for my brothers and sisters all over the world. May we unite to proclaim the good news of salvation to all people. Amen.

Forgiveness – Old Testament

And Joseph said unto them, "Fear not; for am I in the place of God?"

Genesis 50: 6

Joseph's brothers wanted forgiveness after leaving him in a pit alone years earlier, but Joseph knew only a holy God could completely forgive sin, and so he questioned them for asking personal forgiveness.

God says: "I, even I, am he who blotteth out thy transgressions for mine own sake, and will not remember thy sins" (Isaiah 43: 25).

While a person can forgive another for offensive sin, it is still God who provides true forgiveness.

Consider reading King David's path to forgiveness in Psalms 51 after sinning with Uriah's wife, Bathsheba.

David asked for mercy, acknowledged sin, and committed himself to teach other people about God's ways.

The words by God to David's son Solomon may sum up the path to finding forgiveness. "If my people, who are called by my name, shall humble themselves, and pray, and seek my face, and turn from their wicked ways, then will I hear from heaven, and will forgive their sin, and will heal their land" (2 Chronicles 7: 14).

Dear Lord, I humbly confess my sin. Please forgive me and create a new heart within me to serve you in righteousness. Amen

Forgiveness – New Testament

"And when ye stand praying, forgive, if ye have ought against any, that your Father also, who is in heaven, may forgive you your trespasses."
Mark 11: 25

Jesus says the first requirement to being personally forgiven of sin by God is to forgive all other people of their sins.

However, we may have sinned against God himself by failing to put Him first in tithing, activity, and family loyalty.

For these sins to be removed, they must be completely acknowledged and put on the back on God's sinless Son, Jesus.

Christ Jesus is the pure sacrifice for our sins that allows us to become completely forgiven.

The Bible says: If we confess our sins, he is faithful and just to forgive us our sins, and to cleanse us from all unrighteousness (1 John 1: 9-2: 2).

Sin may take years to redeem, but we are encouraged to patiently redeem the time (Ephesians 5: 9-17).

There's no better time than right now to acknowledge sin and enter private prayer to ask forgiveness.

Dear Lord, I confess my sins and abandon them. And I thank you for Christ who takes my sins upon his back to the cross and removes them. Forgiveness is truly with you, and your mercy endures forever. Amen.

Friends – Old Testament

Now when Job's three friends heard of all this evil that was come upon him, they came every one from his own place; Eliphaz the Tenamite, and Bildad the Shuhite, and Zophar the Naamathite: for they had made an appointment together to come to mourn with him and to comfort him. Job 2: 11

Friends came to Job's aid after he suffered loss of family, farm, and health, but Job said, "Miserable comforters are ye all."

Friends don't always understand the problems, but God does, and that's a good reason for getting to know God as a friend.

The Lord spoke to Moses face to face as a man speaketh unto his friend (Exodus 33: 11).

So when difficult times come, commune with God as you would a friend for consolation, guidance, and protection. It is better to trust in the Lord than to put confidence in man (Psalms 118: 8).

For domestic friendship, the Bible says: To have friends, one must show himself friendly and there is a friend who [stays] closer than a brother (Proverbs 18: 24). A true friend loves at all times (Proverbs 17: 17).

But the Bible warns us about people who may not be trustworthy. Trust not in a friend, put not confidence in a guide; keep the doors of thy mouth from her that lieth in thy bosom (Micah 6: 5). And make no friendship with an angry man (Proverbs 22: 24).

May we be reminded though, it was only after Job prayed for his friends, that his captivity was turned away (Job 42: 10).

Dear Father in Heaven, Thank you for friends, but you are my true friend who is with me always. Amen.

Friends – New Testament

If there be therefore any consolation in Christ, if any comfort of love, if any fellowship of the Spirit, if any bowels and mercies, Fulfill ye my joy, that ye be likeminded, having the same love, being of one accord, of one mind. Let nothing be done through strife or vainglory; but in lowliness of mind let each esteem others better than themselves.

Philippians 2: 1-3

Philippians 2: 1-3 gives us advice on how to be a friend and how to treat a friend.

We humble ourselves and listen. We show compassion and mercy. And we fellowship in the spirit of God's truth and love.

Jesus did likewise though he was the Son of God with great power; he humbled himself to be a friend to nearly everyone.

He told his disciples: "Henceforth, I call you not servants; for the servant knoweth not what his lord doeth: but I have called you friends; for all things that I have heard of my Father I have made known unto you" (John 15: 15).

But may we also think about sharing God's love with strangers.

A stranger who needs witness from God will be a friend.

Dear Lord, I humble myself to listen, encourage, and help friends, but I also love Jesus as a friend who is with me forever. Amen.

Gambling – Old Testament

> And Samson said unto them, "I will now put forth a riddle unto you: if ye can certainly declare it me within the seven days of the feast, and find it out, then I will give you thirty sheets, and thirty change of garments."
> Judges 14: 12

Samson gambled that his thirty friends couldn't solve a riddle about a honeycomb being in a lion's carcass, and he lost.

Then he gambled his new wife Delilah couldn't find the source of his strength, but she found out and told a man to shave Samson's hair.

Samson's final gamble came when he pulled down the pillars of an outdoor stadium and lost his life, but he had asked God for permission to avenge his enemies.

Possibly we are on the losing end of a gambling spree but want to save our life.

The only way to do so is commit our assets and ways to God. God already owns all we have but He wants a portion to be returned (Genesis 28: 22; Leviticus 27: 30-34).

And we are not to idolize money: Ye shall not make with me gods of silver, neither shall ye make unto you gods of gold (Exodus 20:22-23).

Serving this stable God should be our first priority in life.

Dear Lord, Thank you for providing my assets. May I invest them for your purpose rather than my selfishness, and I will be in the right place to serve you. Amen.

Gambling – New Testament

"And when he had spent all, there arose a mighty famine in that land, and he began to be in want."
Luke 15: 14

Jesus tells a story about a young man going out and wasting his father's goods with riotous living and then wanting to return home.

Fortunately his father was waiting for him with open arms.

Our outcome may not be as fortunate: parents, family, or friends may reject us because we have gambled away our goods. Friends or family may have suffered, not only from the goods that were lost but from the time and effort spent losing them.

And then we have explaining to do.

But our Father in heaven welcomes us home with mercy when we remorsefully acknowledge wasting assets and ask forgiveness.

He has had mercy upon thousands of people who bow down in humility.

We don't have to gamble to win God's love: it is free for the asking and acceptance of God's Son Christ who takes away sin.

Dear Lord, Thank you for providing Christ who has died for my sin. I confess my gambling sin and promise to commit all my assets to you. Sustain me with provisions I pray. Amen.

Homeless – Old Testament

The Lord is my strength and song, and he is become my salvation; he is my God, and I will prepare him an habitation; my father's God, and I will exalt him.
Exodus 15: 2

Moses glorified God for drowning Pharaoh's army in the Red Sea but Moses also found himself homeless.

His people had left the Egyptian home camp and now were in a wilderness without food or water.

Serving God requires personal sacrifice; nevertheless, the Israelites were sustained in the wilderness and entered a land of milk, honey, and green pastures by their faith and strength.

Consider God in your desire for a good home.

It was only after the people prayed to God for relief that God acted on their behalf to free them from slavery and find a good home.

Dear Lord, You are my true home, but I do ask for shelter where I can be safe and comfortable and give you the glory. Amen.

Homeless – New Testament

"The foxes have holes, and the birds of the air have nests; but the son of man hath not where to lay his head." Matthew 8: 20

Jesus was homeless because he was spreading the word of God around the country and in fear of the rulers who were out to hurt him.

But Jesus did have friends, such as Peter and Zaccheus, and the scriptures indicate that he stayed at their homes.

It's no fun being homeless: there's no place for a bed, chair for comfort, storage for food, and no cleansing facility. It seems like everything is dirty, cold, and lonely.

But there is still communion with God, and a great dependence begins to develop solely on God in prayer.

Jesus said, "Verily I say unto you, There is no man that hath left house, or brethren, or sisters, or father, or mother, or wife, or children, or lands, for my sake, and the gospel's, But he shall receive an hundredfold now in this time, houses, and brethren, and sisters, and mothers, and children, and lands, with persecutions; and in the age to come eternal life" (Mark 10: 29-30).

Acceptance of Jesus brings us into a congregation of many homes and friends. Spiritually, we always have a home knowing the Lord, and we are encouraged by the Apostle Paul, For we know that if our earthly house of this tabernacle is dissolved, we have a building of God (2 Corinthians 5: 1).

Dear Lord, I know you are my eternal home, but I do ask for shelter that I may be able to serve you better and be healthy and protected from the weather. Amen.

Humble – Old Testament

  And thou shalt remember all the way the Lord thy God led thee this forty years in the wilderness, to humble, and to prove thee, to know what was in thine heart, whether thou wouldest keep his commandments or not.
Deuteronomy 8: 2

  Being in the wilderness is a very humbling experience because the weather can be harsh, there's little water, and the trails can be hard to find.
  So we need help, and if it's not being destitute in a forest wilderness, it can be in business, domestic relationships, or personal needs.
  Beginning each day humbly in prayer to God keeps us in the right place.
  The writer of Psalms 69 was humble, poor, sorrowful, reproached by enemies, drowning in waters, hated, ashamed, and had no friends. Yet he praised God with a song and gave thanks.
  The humble shall see this, and be glad; and your heart shall live that seek God (Psalms 69: 32).
  The Bible says: Humility is life (Proverbs 22: 4).

  Dear Lord, "My heart is not haughty, nor mine eyes lofty: neither do I exercise myself in great matters, or in things too high for me. Surely I have behaved and quieted myself, as a child that is weaned of his mother: my soul is even as a weaned child" (Psalms 131). Amen.

Humble – New Testament

"Verily, verily, I say unto you, 'The servant is not greater than his lord; neither he that is sent greater than he that sent him.' If ye know these things, happy are ye if ye do them."

John 13: 16-17

Humility recognizes God is greater than us, and Jesus gives an example by having washed his disciples' feet in John 13: 5.

But many people will not humble themselves before God or other people. Their pride is high, along with their stubbornness and conceit, until they need help and there is no one available.

There is much satisfaction being a humble servant of God. People like to be helped, and humility is good for our health.

The Bible says, God resisteth the proud, but giveth grace unto the humble (James 4: 6).

To be humble, consider fasting from food periodically to know God alone can meet needs. And consider listening more than speaking.

Put on therefore as the elect of God, holy and beloved; tender mercies, kindness, humbleness of mind, meekness, and long-suffering (Colossians 3: 12).

Humility also receives correction, for God loves whom he corrects.

The Bible says this correction allows us to partake of God's holiness and yields the peaceable fruits of righteousness (Hebrews 12: 8-11).

Dear God, Humble me to be more like Jesus, who served the people's needs and was obedient to you. Amen.

Imprisonment – Old Testament

And Joseph's master took him and put him into the prison, a place where the king's prisoners were bound: and he was there in the prison.

Genesis 39: 20

Joseph was falsely accused of adultery with his master's wife and put in a dungeon.

But Joseph kept his faith in God to become free, and one day, he was released for his good prayers.

According to the Psalms, the Lord has the power to free the prisoner (Psalms 146: 7). Psalms 145 and 146 inspires a prisoner to hope in the living God for freedom.

The Lord upholdeth all that fall, and raiseth up all those who are bowed down (Psalms 145: 14).

Imprisonment is a terrible, lonely experience.

No one can be trusted. The rooms are small. The activities are scheduled. Some prisoners are insane. And there is little communication from loved ones outside of prison.

Meanwhile, we are to be faithful, thank the Lord for each day, stay in prayer, and give testimony of God's presence, correction, and guidance to become free.

Dear Father in Heaven, This jail is dreadful, yet I know you have the power to give me freedom: I also call upon your name in truth, love, mercy, and wisdom to protect me. Amen.

Imprisonment – New Testament

Are they ministers of Christ? (I speak as a fool) I am more: in labors more abundant, in stripes above measure, in prisons more frequently, in deaths often.
2 Corinthians 11: 23

The Apostle Paul was a prisoner for Christ's sake but many of us are prisoners because we disobeyed the law; however, the law is our schoolmaster that brings us to know Christ (Galatians 3: 24).

Being in prison is a good time for thinking about what we have done to get there -- and repenting of the crime (if we are guilty).

And in the New Testament, we have some guidance on how to act: Repent, therefore, and be converted, that your sins may be blotted out, when the time of refreshing shall come from the presence of the Lord. And he shall send Jesus Christ, who before was preached unto you (The Acts 3: 19-20),

Christ Jesus has passed through the veil of darkness to give us access to God and light upon our confession of sin to become free (Hebrews 6: 18: 19).

Experiencing this new birth and freedom in Christ makes us want share the story.

The Apostle Paul shared the gospel of salvation with a keeper of the prison, and he became saved (Acts 16: 19).

Christ said he came "to preach deliverance to the captives and set at liberty those who are bruised" (Luke 4: 18).

Dear Father in Heaven, I Thank you for your wonderful word of life. You give me hope in Christ – having a friend I can trust. Protect me I pray. Amen.

Jealousy – Old Testament

And Saul eyed David, from that day and forward.
1 Samuel 18: 9

Saul became jealous of David after David killed a giant named Goliath and became a hero among the people. And then Saul chased David all around the country trying to kill him.

Saul admitted later he had been foolish and made a mistake chasing David (1 Samuel 26: 21). But it was a terrible error because David prayed for God to have vengeance, and Saul was eventually killed in a battle.

We don't want to become the objects of someone's vengeance prayer because of jealousy. We should want to draw close to God in devotion and share the unique gift of the spirit that he has given.

If we know God, we should not become jealous of anyone or anything: it is God whom we love first in obedience to His First Commandment: Thou shalt have no other gods before me (Exodus 20: 3).

But God does have a right to be jealous. He becomes jealous of us when we worship anything or anyone other than Him (Deuteronomy 32: 21); and He will correct us to know He is God.

Dear Lord, I abandon jealousy to worship and put you first in my life. I am content to serve you in righteousness, mercy, and truth. Amen.

Jealousy – New Testament

If ye then be risen with Christ, seek those things which are above, where Christ sitteth on the right hand of God. Set your affection on things above, not on things on the earth.

Colossians 3: 1-2

It's easy to become jealous of other people that may abundant possessions, wonderful personalities, or have a multitude of friends.

But we are warned: Let us not be desirous of vain glory, provoking one another, envying one another (Galatians 5: 26).

Consider Christ who had no reputation, worldly title, expensive clothes, or personal assets.

If there is any reason to emulate someone, it is Jesus Christ who knew no sin, served other people, quoted God's word of life, and spoke truth in the midst of a hopeless generation.

And now he is risen into the heavens.

Our focus should be on Jesus -- conforming more to the image of this heavenly Savior who is able to intercede for us (Romans 8: 29; 12: 1-16).

Each of us who confesses Christ is considered by God to have a unique gift of the spirit, and we should employ it to the glory of God (1 Corinthians 12: 11).

Dear Lord, Humble me so that I am not envious of anyone of anything. You are my life, but I do thank you for my friends in Christ Jesus. Amen.

Joyfulness – Old Testament

And he will love thee, and bless thee, and multiply thee; he will also bless the fruit of thy womb, and the fruit of thy land.
Deuteronomy 7: 13

Happiness in the Old Testament is defined as obeying God's laws and loving him with all thine heart, mind, soul, and strength (Deuteronomy 6-8; 28: 1-14).

But there will be troubles to pursuing happiness, for sickness, enemies, sin, slander, or hunger may get in the way.

Yet God has power over these hindrances, and we need only trust and obey Him.

The Bible says in Psalms 37: 3-4: Trust in the Lord, and do good; so shalt thou dwell in the land, and verily thou shalt be fed. Delight thyself also in the Lord, and he shall give thee the desires of thine heart.

Our plans are doomed to fail but God's plans have proved to work despite the hardships.

Consider acknowledging God in your life and following His plan for happiness.

The wise man Solomon summarizes happiness by saying there is nothing better for a man to eat, drink, be merry, live joyfully with the wife, and enjoy his work (Ecclesiastes 9: 7-9).

Dear Lord, I thank you for being here. Your joy is truly my strength. I confess my sins and free my mind to work and glorify you. Amen.

Joyfulness – New Testament

And the angel said unto them, "Fear not: for, behold, I bring you good tidings of great joy, which shall be to all people."

Luke 2: 10

The shepherds became joyful when they heard the good news of Christ's birth, so they immediately went to Bethlehem to see the child, and upon seeing the newborn Savior, they returned home praising and glorifying God.

The righteous man, Simeon, was also joyful, and he held the baby in his arms and blessed God. Simeon had waited long for the consolation of Israel.

And Christ's mother, Mary, said a lengthy prayer that praised God: "My soul doth magnify the Lord. And my spirit hath rejoiced in God my Savior. For he hath regarded the low estate of his handmaiden; for, behold, from henceforth all generations shall call me blessed" (Luke 2: 46-27).

Christ is a risen Savior who frees us from sin and allows us to enter the joy of our Father in heaven. He was born for our salvation and it gives us happiness to know him.

"And now come I to thee; and these things I speak in the world, that they might have my joy fulfilled in themselves" (John 17: 13).

Dear Father in Heaven, It was for joy Jesus was born to take away sin. Thank you for releasing me of sin to have pure joy on earth. Amen.

Loneliness –Old Testament

And the Lord God said, "It is not good that the man should be alone: I will make him a help meet for him."

Genesis 2: 18

Loneliness is the primary reason why God put a man and woman together.

However, some people are called to be separate, such as the Nazarene, who vowed a vow of separation unto God (Numbers 6).

Also, a eunuch was encouraged to not think of being like a dry tree, but the Lord says they have a place within his walls and house (Isaiah 56: 3-5).

During a feeling of loneliness, make sure your relationship with God is intact (Read Psalm 81).

God has promised to be with us regardless of our status in the world if we love and obey Him.

Also, consider fellowshipping with other believers.

The Bible says, Bless ye God in the congregations, even the Lord, from the fountain of Israel (Psalms 68: 26).

Dear Lord, This loneliness is a good time to learn more about your word. I praise you for being here and I thank you for other believers who also worship you. Amen.

Loneliness – New Testament

"... I will never leave thee, nor forsake thee."
Hebrews 13: 5

God is always with us if we have turned to him in prayer, called on his name, confessed our sins, and become forgiven.

But if we don't know God, we are indeed alone: we are like the branches without a vine as Jesus described in John 15: 1-6. And those branches were thrown into the fire and burned.

Confessing Jesus, who is like a vine that provides a path to God (John 14: 23); we become one with the Lord and have communion.

Now, therefore, ye are no more strangers and sojourners, but fellow citizens with the saints, and of the household of God (Ephesians 2: 19).

And we are encouraged to fellowship with believers in the congregation (Hebrews 10: 25), and entertain strangers as witness for the Lord (Hebrews 13: 1).

But Jesus treasured time alone with God in the desert, mountain cave, seaside, and garden.

Praising and pleasing God in private confirms we are not alone.

Dear Lord, I praise you for being here in my loneliness, and I thank you for Jesus who died for my sin. May my loneliness be turned into joy with the Holy Spirit and others who praise you. Amen.

Lost – Old Testament

Now for a long season, Israel had been without the true God, and without a teaching priest, and without law.
2 Chronicles 15: 3

There was no peace in the land. Nations were destroying nations, cities were destroying cites, and great vexations were occurring.

The people of Israel were lost because they had turned away from God's law and started acquiring abominable idols. And the temple altar was in disrepair.

So God sent Azania the prophet to meet King Asa of Israel and said, "The Lord is with you while you are with him; and if ye seek him, he will be found by you . . ." (2 Chronicles 15: 2).

So King Asa put away all the golden images and abominable idols that were defiling the land, and he repaired the altar of the Lord.

The people returned to the law of God with all their heart and soul.

Establishing a covenant with God begins a journey to become found and have peace.

But it's up to us to call on God and repent from vain work, and it sometimes takes getting lost.

Dear Lord, I praise you for being here in my lost condition. You are my home and faith, and I come to you for rest and guidance: grant me peace, rest, and happiness. Amen.

Lost -- New Testament

"For the Son of Man is come to save that which was lost."

Matthew 18: 11

That what Jesus does for us -- allows us to be at home with God and come back into the congregation of believers.

But many people have fallen victim to false doctrine and been led astray.

The Bible says that some shall depart from the faith, giving heed to seducing spirits, and doctrines of devils (1Timothy 4: 1).

When you feel lost, consider humbling yourself and seeking Jesus with your whole heart.

Upon acceptance of Christ, there is direction for living, a purpose for each day, and a peace that exceeds all understanding.

Furthermore, we find truth, because Jesus says, "I am the way, the truth, and the life (John 14: 6).

And Christ commands us to love the Lord thy God with all thy heart, and with all thy soul, and with all thy mind, and with all thy strength – and thy neighbor as thyself (Mark 12: 30-31).

God is an anchor for our souls (Hebrews 6: 19).

Dear Lord, Life is so confusing, but I trust you to keep me safe. May I have peace, rest, and joy. Amen.

Love – Old Testament

"Where thou diest, will I die, and there will I be buried; the Lord do so to me, and more also if anything but death part thee and me."
Ruth 1: 17

Ruth gives us a wonderful example of love when she vows to stay by her mother-in-law Naomi's side until death.

Our love should be as strong, but our first love should be for God.

God commands us: And thou shalt love the Lord thy God with all thine heart, and with all thy soul, and with all thy might (Deuteronomy 6: 5).

Once we understand the love of God, then we know how to share God's love.

The Bible says: Thou shalt not avenge, nor bear any grudge against the children of thy people, but thou shalt love thy neighbor as thyself. I am the Lord (Leviticus 19: 18).

Ruth returned with Naomi to her homeland and was rewarded with rest when she married Boaz.

Dear Lord, I love you with all my heart, mind, soul, and strength. May I set an example of love towards others with humble service that glorifies you and produces good and merciful work. Amen.

Love – New Testament

"This is my commandment, that ye love one another, as I have loved you."
John 15: 12

These are the departing words from Jesus to his disciples before he went to die for the sins of humanity – to love one another.

But many of us have problems loving one another either because we don't understand the characteristics of love or haven't forgiven someone of sin.

The acceptance of Christ renews our lives, and puts us in the right spirit to love.

Therefore, if any man be in Christ, he is a new creation; old things are passed away; behold, all things are become new (2 Corinthians 5: 17).

Consider looking at 1 Corinthians 13: 4-8 and the sixteen characteristics of love: love should flow naturally from the heart but these characteristics help start the process. Think about each item and how you can apply it to real life.

Love is patient, and kind. Love is not envious, vain, puffed up, indecent, nor does it pursue its own way.

It is not easily provoked, thinks no evil, does not rejoice over wrong but rejoices with the truth, and quietly covers all things.

Love believes, hopes, and endures all things.
Love never fails.

Dear God, May I show the love that Jesus did when he went and helped people, but may I also share the good news of salvation. Amen.

Lying – Old Testament

And Jacob said unto his father, "I am Esau, thy first-born; I have done according to thou badest me: arise, I pray thee, sit, and eat of my venison, that thy soul may bless me."
Genesis 27: 19

Jacob lied to his nearly blind father about being Esau so he would get his older brother's blessing.

We may lie to get something we want, or try to be something we aren't, but God will confront our lies because He loves us enough to correct us.

He confronted Jacob in a private place where an angel wrestled Jacob to the ground and wounded his thigh.

God forbid it takes an injury before we tell the truth but usually something bad happens before we confess it.

The Bible says: Thou shalt not bear false witness against thy neighbor (Exodus 20: 16); and thou shalt not raise a false report (Exodus 23: 1).

Lying hurts the innocent person and the liar.

We might consider the Lord hates lying (Proverbs 6: 16-17).

The lip of truth shall be established forever, but a lying tongue is but for a moment (Proverbs 12: 19).

Dear Lord, Forgive me for lying and have mercy on me. May I tell the truth and my apology be accepted. Amen.

Lying – New Testament

But Peter said, "Ananias, why hath Satan filled thine heart to lie to the Holy Ghost, and to keep back part of the price of the land?"

Acts 5: 3

Apostle Ananias lied to other apostles about his wealth being put in the common treasury.

When Ananias was confronted by the Holy Spirit, he was struck dead (Acts 5: 1-5).

Rather than face God's harsh judgment for lying, we should come to the truth right now: we are sinners who need Christ Jesus to help us understand who we are and to tell the truth in every matter (Ephesians 4: 21-29).

The Bible says: Wherefore putting away lying, speak every man truth with his neighbor; for we are members one of another (Ephesians 4: 25).

Consider also reading Colossians 3: 5-17 for living a life of truth.

Dear Father in Heaven, Forgive me for lying, and help me confess the truth. I praise you for Jesus who died for my sin to let me live in truth. Amen.

Marriage – Old Testament

And Abraham said unto his eldest servant of his house that ruled over all that he had, "Put, I pray thee, thy hand under my thigh; and I will make thee swear by the Lord, the God of heavens, and the God of all the earth, that thou shalt not take a wife unto my son of the daughters of the Canaanites, among whom I dwell."

Genesis 24: 2-3

The servant was instructed to go find a wife for Abraham's son Isaac among God's own people.

As men, we might look among God's people for a kind woman, because there is an agreement of faith and belief that God is the priority for life.

The servant sat by a well of water, and when the maiden Rebekah came along and offered him and the animals water, the servant took this as a sign from God that Rebekah was to be the wife of Isaac.

Women might be kind to strangers and discerning to find out more about a prospective husband, as Rebekah did when she asked her family.

After being questioned by Rebekah's family, the servant was allowed to take Rebekah home to Isaac.

But the most important principle is that God is the true maker for marriage.

Rebekah and her husband Isaac both loved God and were rewarded with children, wealth, and togetherness.

Dear Lord, I look to you for the right mate in my life, but first I want to make sure my own spiritual house is in order. Forgive my sin and bring me into a right relationship with you. Amen.

Marriage – New Testament

Husbands, love your wives, even as Christ also loved the church, and gave himself for it.
Ephesians 5: 25

Christ sets a wonderful example of marriage when he gave himself to the church.

Scripture suggests that a husband do likewise by giving himself to the wife.

And women are to follow and be receptive to the husband's needs; yet look to the Lord for blessing.

And their relationship becomes strengthened by trust and faith.

Where there is fault, forgive one another, as God in His abundant mercy, has forgiven us (Ephesians 4: 32).

Christ is the true bond for marriage because he takes away sin, intercedes in problems, and provides a path to oneness in God.

Finally, be ye all of one mind, having compassion one of another; love as brethren, be pitiful, be courteous (1 Peter 3: 8). (Consider reading the full text of Peter's advice for married couples in 1 Peter 3: 1-12.)

Marriage is honorable in all, and the bed becomes undefiled (Hebrews 13: 4).

Dear Lord, I praise you for my marriage. May our lives be of grace, peace, righteousness, love, mercy, and happiness. Amen.

Mercy – Old Testament

The Lord is merciful and gracious, slow to anger, and plenteous in mercy.
Psalms 103: 8

There are ten traits of mercy in Psalms 103.

The Lord forgives sins, heals diseases, redeems life from destruction, covers with love and tenderness, and puts good words in our mouths.

Our youth is renewed. There is righteousness and judgment for the oppressed.

Mercy is higher than the heavens; sin is removed forever; and mercy is everlasting.

How wonderful it is to know we can enjoy all these mercies!

But they are dependent on a few items: the reverential fear of God, keeping His covenant, and performing the commandments,

Remember, when God visits our sins, he promises us mercy in Exodus 20: 6: showing mercy unto thousands of them that love me, and keep my commandments.

God's mercy endures forever if we are obedient and faithful to God.

Dear Father in Heaven, Thank you for providing these mercies, May each of us obey your word and your commandments to receive mercy. Amen.

Mercy – New Testament

"Blessed are the merciful, for they shall obtain mercy."
Matthew 5: 7

Jesus teaches us that if we show mercy to others, we will receive mercy.

And he gave us a good example in the parable of a Samaritan in Luke 10:33, who helped bind up a man's wounds and furnished money for his care.

Remember, God was merciful to us as sinners to provide Jesus as a sacrifice for our sins (Hebrews 10: 28). The least we can do is show God's mercy for other people and help them.

Being merciful to another person helps in work, forgives a debt, gives a gift, or sends words of encouragement.

And we can be merciful to ourselves -- taking care of our bodies with good nutrition, cleansing, and rest.

The scriptures encourage this: for ye are bought with a price; therefore, glorify God in your body and in your spirit, which are God's (1 Corinthians 6: 20).

Many people wonder why they are chosen by God.

The Bible says: So then, it is not of him that willeth, nor of him that runneth, but of God that showeth mercy (Romans 9: 16).

Dear Father in Heaven, I thank you for Jesus who suffered for me and took my sins to the cross of death. May I tell others about this merciful act so they will know your compassion. Amen.

Money – Old Testament

And if thy way be too long for thee, so that thou art not able to carry it . . . then shalt thou turn it into money, and bind up the money in thine hand, and shalt go unto the place which the Lord thy God shall choose.
Deuteronomy 14: 24-25

Money is a component God incorporated to lessen our load, not make it heavier.

If we have some extra, we should increase tithes to the Lord, invest in the market for his glory, or distribute liberally to the poor.

What we are not to do is hoard money.

The Bible says, There is a sore evil which I have seen under the sun, namely, riches kept for the owners thereof to their hurt . . . (Ecclesiastes 5: 13-14).

King Solomon had a great attitude when it came to thinking about money: he prayed first for righteousness, wisdom, and spiritual blessings.

As a result, God gave him monetary riches (2 Chronicles 1: 11-12).

And when Solomon did become rich, his wealth was used to build a temple dedicated to God.

Dear Lord, I put you first in life and I trust you to supply my needs. May my assets be invested for your purpose and for your kingdom. Amen.

Money – New Testament

"No man can serve two masters; for either he will hate the one, and love the other; or else he will hold to the one, and despise the other. Ye cannot serve God and [money]."

Matthew 6: 24

God doesn't take second place to a desire for money.

He is a jealous God who knows what is best for us.

And so Jesus says to lay up treasures in heaven where moth does not eat them away nor rust destroys it, and thieves can not steal (Matthew 6: 19-20).

Serve the kingdom of God first, and he will add such things as we need (Matthew 6: 33).

Serving God first performs righteous work, helps people, and shows mercy.

We are not totally precluded from trying to make a lot of money; we are just expected to invest it for God's sake (see parable of the long journey; Luke 19: 23).

Consider beginning each day with a prayer that wants to serve God in the spirit.

God is a rewarder to those that believe in Him (Hebrews 11: 6).

But we should all be in remembrance of the popular verse: For the love of money is the root of all evil . . . (1Timothy 6: 10).

.Dear Father in Heaven, you are my first desire, and I commit my way to you. Thank you for providing my riches in Christ Jesus and my daily bread. Amen.

Obedience – Old Testament

Now the word of the Lord came unto Jonah, the son of Amittai, saying, Arise, go to Nineveh, that great city, and cry against it: for their wickedness is come up before me. But Jonah rose up to flee unto Tarshish from the presence of the Lord.

Jonah 1: 1-3

Jonah knew what he was supposed to do and where he was supposed to go -- but he went the opposite way.

That's what we do sometimes: the Lord wants us to do something or go somewhere but we go the opposite way.

Jonah found himself in the middle of a big storm on a sinking boat with an angry crew for disobeying God's command, and then the crew decided to get rid of him by sending him into the water.

We do not want to experience God's harsh discipline for being disobedient.

That means if God has given us a mission, there's no choice but to follow through with it.

And we might remember, to obey is better than the giving of many offerings (1 Samuel 15: 22).

Dear Lord, It is difficult to obey, but I choose to be humble and obedient. Bless me Lord as I faithfully endure your word for life and carry out Your mission. Amen.

Obedience – New Testament

And being found in fashion as a man, he humbled himself and became obedient, unto death, even the death of the cross.

Philippians 2: 8

God's son Christ sets a wonderful example of obedience when he received a command to die for the people's sins and went to the cross of death.

Though our purpose is to live and show God's glory performing good works, we should do so knowing God has something better in heaven reserved for us (Hebrews 12: 2).

However, the apostle Peter was threatened with jail for obeying God and preaching Christ in front of non-believing rulers.

Peter and the other apostles said, "We ought to obey God rather than men" (Acts 5: 29).

The apostles knew the power of Jesus could set people free from sin and heal the sick, and it was their decision to tell the world.

But there are times to obey those who have authority over us, so that they will give a good report (Hebrews 13: 17).

Dear Father in Heaven, Christ's obedience inspires me to follow your calling and do it with joy, knowing that I too will be delivered into something better. May I indeed fulfill the mission of presenting Christ as Savior to the world. Amen.

Patience – Old Testament

And Jacob served seven years for Rachel: and they seemed unto him but a few days, for the love he had to her.

Genesis 29: 20

Jacob waited fourteen years to marry Rachel because Uncle Laban deceitfully gave him Leah to marry seven years earlier.

So Jacob had to have lots of patience, but he didn't sit idle: he multiplied his cattle to become rich.

While being patient for one thing to happen that God has ordained, we might get busy on something else that gives God glory.

What we are not to do while being patient is to hasten after and serve another god, while waiting for the promise (Psalms 16: 4).

Consider the prayer of the psalmist: My soul, wait thou upon God; for my expectation is from Him (Psalm 62: 5).

So during troubled times, we are encouraged to be patient.

We are to patiently trust God for all things (Psalms 37).

Dear Lord, Your patience is infinite, and while I wait for your promise to come true, I will continue to work for your glory. Amen.

Patience – New Testament

For ye have need of patience, that, after ye have done the will of God, ye might receive the promise.
Hebrews 10: 36

The promise that we receive one day is being able to rest from all our works that have been accomplished upon earth (Revelation 14: 12-13).

Until that time, we are encouraged to perform God's will *patiently* (James 5: 7-18; 1 Peter 2: 20).

The writer James gave us a good illustration of how a farmer had patience in James 5: 7: Behold, the farmer, waiteth for the precious fruit of the earth, and hath long patience for it, until he receive the early and latter rain.

The farmer had faith that his crops would grow and would now have patience.

But he would not have sit around idle: he would have tore down weeds, got rid of pests, and sharpened his tools for the harvest.

There are always projects to do while waiting on a promise.

Dear Lord, Your patience is everlasting and I wait upon you to receive the promise. May I be productive for your sake. Amen.

Peace – Old Testament

And there was a strife between the headsmen of Abram's cattle and the herdsmen of Lot's cattle: and the Canaanite and Perizzite dwelt then in the land.
                                                              Genesis 13: 7

Abram and Lot's herdsmen were about to fight over grazing land for their animals, so Abram called a meeting on a trailhead overlooking a vast amount of land. And the two men came to an agreement: Lot would occupy one part while Abram the other.
But it was Lot who chose first.
Lot chose the plains of Jordan to live, but it turned out to be a bad decision because the people were wicked, and God would create havoc on the town to destroy it.
When there is a disagreement with someone, it may mean yielding to the other person.
We also need personal peace with God
He has promised: And I will give peace in the land, and ye shall lie down, and none shall make you afraid; and I will rid evil beasts out of the land, neither shall the sword go through your land (Leviticus 26: 6).
This peace comes by faith and obedience to God's statutes and laws.

Dear Lord, I humble myself from fighting and arguing, and I seek the peace that comes from you. The battle is yours Lord. Amen.

Peace – New Testament

"Peace I leave with you, my peace I give unto you; not as the world giveth, give I unto you. Let not your heart be troubled, neither let it be afraid."
John 14: 27

Jesus is able to give us peace because takes away sin and provides a path to God.

But many of us think peace is at a beach, forest, or mountain stream.

While these places give us environmental peace by the absence of sound, true emotional peace comes from agreement with God through Jesus Christ (Romans 5: 1).

In Mark 5: 1-20, a man had no peace; he was hurting himself and could not be restrained, but after he met Jesus, he was found sitting in his right mind.

That's what Jesus can do – take away emotional conflicts to give peace.

But domestically, Jesus did not come to bring peace but division -- knowing his new testament would separate the people (Luke 12: 51-53).

Yet the Apostle Paul said that Jesus has established peace -- by breaking down the middle wall of partition between the Jews and Gentiles (Ephesians 2: 13-16).

Dear Lord, Knowing you gives me peace, and I thank you for Jesus providing the way. Amen.

Persecution – Old Testament

And the officers of the children of Israel, whom Pharaoh's task makers had set over them, were beaten . . . .

Exodus 5: 14

The officers were beaten because their subordinates could not keep up with a workload Pharaoh's slave masters' kept increasing.

So one day, the children of Israel left the Egyptian camp, not only to get away from persecution but serve God in a holy land.

Persecution may increase our workload or try to stop us from worshipping God. It may even defame or try to kill us, but God still promises to be with us.

God drowned Pharaoh's army and chariots in the Red Sea while the children of Israel crossed safely to the other side (Exodus 14: 28).

Moses remembered the persecution the people had endured, and said: the Lord thy God will put all these curses upon thine enemies, and on them that hate thee, who persecuted thee (Deuteronomy 30: 7).

In the midst of persecution, our primary responsibility is to God, to witness for Him and proclaim His name (Deuteronomy 4: 14-20).

Dear Lord, "O Lord my God, in thee do I put my trust; save me from all those who persecute me, and deliver me;" Psalm 7: 1. Amen.

Persecution – New Testament

> Yea and all that will live godly in Christ Jesus shall suffer persecution.
> 2 Timothy 3: 12

Living godly in Christ Jesus exposes us to persecution because we have cleaned up our lives and the devil loves nothing better to want a part of it – without having to bow down to God..

Our defense is prayer: Praying always with prayer and supplication in the Spirit, and watching thereunto with all perseverance and supplication for all saints (Ephesians 6: 18).

The Apostle Paul says that he was persecuted at Antioch, Iconium, and Lystra, but the Lord saved him from them all.

However, the Apostle Stephen, who was accused of subverting the law and slandering Moses, was stoned to death (Acts 6: 9-7: 60).

"Behold, I see the heavens opened, and the son of man standing on the right hand side of God" (Acts 7: 56).

When persecutions come, look to Jesus who sits on the right hand side of God, for he is able to intercede for us.

Be strong in the Lord, and in the power of His might (Ephesians 6: 10).

And we are to be blameless, such as the archangel Michael who did not accuse Satan but said, "The Lord rebukes thee" (Jude 1: 9).

Prayer of Jesus: "But I say unto you, Love your enemies, bless them that curse you, do good to them that hate you, and pray for them which despitefully use you, and persecute you" (Matthew 5: 44).

Prayer – Old Testament

Now when Daniel knew that the writing was signed, he went into his house, and his windows being open in his chamber toward Jerusalem, he kneeled upon his knees three times a day, and prayed and gave thanks before his God, as he did aforetime.
Daniel 6: 10

Daniel went up to his room and prayed towards Jerusalem because he knew God supplied his needs, even after King Darius signed a decree for all men to come to the king when they needed something,

God's temple is open to us, but we must humble ourselves as Daniel and get on our knees.

However, we are warned, God hears the prayer of the righteous (Proverbs 15: 29), but will not hear a prayer of iniquity (Psalms 66: 18).

Therefore, our prayers are to be sincere and righteous according to the laws of God, which are contained in the Holy Scriptures.

But we shouldn't wait for problems to develop before praying.

The prayerful man David gives a good example of when to pray, "Evening, and morning, and at noon, will I pray, and cry aloud, and he shall hear my voice" (Psalms 55: 17).

Dear Lord, I praise you for being here and listening to my petitions. You are a true God that fulfills the prayers of the righteous. Amen.

Prayer -- New Testament

"But thou, when thou prayest, enter into thy closet, and when thou hast shut thy door, pray to thy Father, who is in secret; and thy Father, who seeth in secret, shall reward thee openly."
Matthew 6: 6

    Going into a closed room and being able to commune with the almighty God through Jesus Christ is the greatest gift ever given to man.
    When troubles come, God is here to fix them. When sickness comes, God is here to heal. When evil comes, God is here with righteousness. And when there's a temptation to sin, God is here with Jesus to help us overcome it.
    Jesus exhorts us saying, "And all things, whatever ye shall ask in prayer, believing, ye shall receive" (Matthew 21: 22).
    So we must be careful what we ask for – to make sure it is God's will and not our own. Does the petition give glory to God?
    The Bible also says: For the eyes of the Lord are over the righteous, and his ears are open unto their prayers; but the face of the Lord is against them that do evil (1 Peter 3: 12).

    Dear Father in Heaven, I love you and thank you for the sacrifice of Jesus who allows me to commune with you in prayer. Amen.

Pride -- Old Testament

And if ye will not yet for all this hearken unto me, then I will punish you seven times more for your sin. And I will break the pride of your power; and I will make your heaven as iron, and your earth as bronze, And your strength shall be spent in vain; for your land shall not yield her increase, neither shall the trees of the land yield their fruits. Leviticus 26: 18-20

Selfish pride leads to destruction in front of a holy God.

Consider King Nebuchadnezzar who had proudly exclaimed he had built his kingdom by his power; but as he spoke, a voice came from heaven telling him that his kingdom would be cut down (Daniel 4: 30-21).

When pride gets high like Nebuchadnezzar, God will break it, because God wants his glory for performing good work.

The Bible says, Pride goeth before destruction, and a haughty spirit before a fall (Proverbs 16: 18). When pride comes, then cometh shame (Proverbs 11: 2). A man's pride bringeth him low (Proverbs 29: 23).

Nebuchadnezzar was driven to live with the beasts of the fields, but after being humbled, Nebuchadnezzar praised and declared God was just and truthful.

The fear of the Lord is to hate evil, pride, and arrogance, and the evil way, and the perverse mouth, do I hate (Proverbs 8: 13).

"Nor by might, and not by power, but by my spirit, saith the Lord" (Zechariah 4: 6).

Dear Lord, Forgive me for being so prideful, and humble me to know you better. Amen.

Pride – New Testament

    For all that is in the world, the lust of the flesh, and the lust of the eyes, and the pride of life, is not of the Father, but of the world. And the world passeth away, and the lust of it; but he that doeth the will of God abideth forever.
1 John 2: 16-17

    God is to be given the credit for all our good works, for without him, we can do nothing.

    For we are his workmanship, created in Christ Jesus unto good works, which God hath before ordained that we should walk in them (Ephesians 2: 10).

    The Apostle Paul suggests we be humble -- to walk worthy of the vocation we are called, with all lowliness and meekness, with long-suffering, forbearing one another in love (Ephesians 4: 1-2).

    Believers in Christ do not have to prove anything to anyone or strive to be something they aren't, but simply give God the glory and witness in all actions.

    The Bible also says; Let nothing be done through strife or vain glory . . . (Philippians 2: 3).

    Dear Father in Heaven, I abandon selfish pride to be humble and serve you. Amen.

Purpose – Old Testament

"And, behold, I purpose to build a house unto the name of the Lord my God, as the Lord spake unto David my father, saying, 'Thy son, whom I will set upon they throne in thy room, he shall build a house unto my name.' "

1 Kings 5: 5

God's purpose for Solomon was to build a temple where people could worship.

After construction was finished, a great feast was enjoyed and a sermon was preached that glorified God (1 Kings 8: 12-66).

Fulfilling God's purpose gives us great joy because we are pleasing the very God who created us.

But fulfilling a selfish purpose will lead to a spiritual void. King Solomon's heart was later turned away from God because he had a consortium of concubines.

The Bible says: Blessed is the man whom thou choosest, and causeth to approach unto thee . . . (Psalms 65: 4).

May we understand God's purpose and give Him glory.

Our lives will be complete working for the living God.

Dear Lord, I thank you for drawing me closer to you. May I experience the joy of serving you. Amen.

Purpose – New Testament

That the God of our Lord Jesus Christ, the Father of glory, may give unto you the spirit of wisdom and revelation in the knowledge of him, the eyes of your understanding being enlightened; that ye may know what is the hope of his calling, and what the riches of the glory of his inheritance in the saints.
                                            Ephesians 1: 17-18

The basic purpose of life is to witness Jesus Christ and give God glory.

Jesus knew this, and he relished fulfilling God's purpose.

Jesus gives us a great example of glorifying God in life when he preached the gospel to the poor, healed the brokenhearted, preached deliverance to the captives, gave sight to the blind, and set at liberty them that were bruised (Luke 4: 18).

To find purpose, consider the scripture in John 14: 23: Jesus answered and said unto him, "If a man love me, he will keep my words; and my Father will love him, and we will come unto him, and make our abode with him".

Consider what talent you have to glorify and work for God.

When you find purpose, you find life.

Dear Lord, Thank you for giving me a purpose to live. May I use the spiritual gifts you've given me to glorify your presence and do good work. Amen.

Rejected – Old Testament

The stone which the builders refused is become the head stone of the corner. This is the Lord's doing; it is marvelous in our eyes.
Psalms 118: 22

A stone mason often rejects a rock because it does not fit in the straight line of a wall, but when he gets to the corner of the wall, it fits.

Life can be like that: there's rejection in one place but acceptance in another.

But rather than sit around depressed after being rejected, it is a good time to get busy and find something to do that pleases God.

Consider going to God in prayer and accepting a place of divine service.

There won't be any hardships, worry, or fear, because living and working for God is the ultimate purpose in life.

Dear Lord, I have been rejected, but I know you accept me. I humbly bow before you and trust you to guide me to a better place . Amen.

Rejected – New Testament

"The stone the builders rejected is become the head of the corner."
Mark 12: 10

A friend of mine applied for a job and was rejected because he didn't have enough experience.

Despondently leaving the interview area, he got into his car to drive home but decided to stop off at the local library to get some books.

As he entered the parking lot area gate, an attendant stuck his head out the window to give a lot ticket and asked how things were going.

My friend said, "I'm disappointed because I was rejected for a job I really wanted."

The attendant said, "Well, God can take the 'd' in disappointment and make it a capital 'H' for His appointment".

The man never forgot the words of the parking attendant.

When we are rejected for one thing in the world, God is accepting us for something better.

In a few weeks, the man got a job he loved.

So after rejection, we need patience to wait upon God.

Dear Father in Heaven, May this disappointment be turned into your appointment. Thank you for eliminating undesirable things from my life. Amen.

Repentance – Old Testament

"I have heard thee by the hearing of the ear, but now my eye seeth thee; wherefore I abhor myself, and repent in dust and ashes."

Job 42: 5-6

Repentance for Job took place in ashes and dust when he met God face to face.

That's what repentance does: drives a person to the ground because of shame and dishonor in front of a righteous God.

But Job first tried to justify his actions by talking to his friends.

Friends may share ideas about how to find God, but true repentance convicts the conscience in a private ceremony with a righteous and merciful God.

It's a mystical moment when the holiness of God meets the sins of man – where power meets submission – and peace meets peace.

The psalmist wrote: The sorrows of death compassed me, and the pains of sheol got hold upon me; I found trouble and sorrow. Then called I upon the name of the Lord: O Lord, I beseech thee, deliver my soul (Psalms 116: 3-4).

I will take the cup of salvation and call upon the name of the Lord (Psalms 116: 13).

Dear Lord, I acknowledge my sin and want to change. Humble me, O God – to know your will for my life. Amen.

Repentance – New Testament

When Jesus heard it, he saith unto them, "They that are whole have no need of the physician; but they that are sick. I came not to call the righteous, but sinners to repentance."

Mark 2: 11

Jesus is still calling sinners to repentance because he loves everyone and wants them spared the punishment of sin.

An American Indian preacher I once knew best illustrated repentance when he walked across the church stage only to stop at the far end.

He said, "Before you go the other way, you have to stop. Repentance is the same way. You stop doing wrong and start doing right."

Then he proceeded to walk back to the center of the stage.

Consider stopping in front of God to acknowledge your sin and proceed on to righteousness and truth. That's repentance.

Jesus illustrated how we should act upon repentance when he called a small child out of a crowd and said, "Except ye be converted and become as little children, ye shall not enter into the kingdom of heaven" (Matthew 18: 3).

Dear Father in Heaven, I know I'm doing wrong and I humble myself before you to change. Forgive my sin I pray and allow me to live righteously in Christ Jesus. Amen.

Righteousness – Old Testament

> ... What mean the testimonies, and the statutes, and the judgments, which the Lord our God that commanded you? Then thou shalt say unto thy son, we were Pharaoh's bondmen in Egypt; and the Lord brought us out of Egypt with a mighty hand.
> Deuteronomy 6: 20-21

God's laws had the power to free the Israelites from slavery, but they are also designed to help us find God.

The Bible says: The law of the Lord is perfect, converting the soul; the testimony of the Lord is sure, making wise the simple. The statutes of the Lord are right, rejoicing the heart; the commandment of the Lord is pure, enlightening the eyes (Psalms 19: 7-8).

Consider also reading Psalm 1, which speaks of two men and two ways: one man seeks the righteousness of God and becomes stable and successful – while the ungodly man is blown away like chaff in the wind.

The Biblical books of the Law are considered to be Genesis, Exodus, Leviticus, Numbers, and Deuteronomy.

God's Old Testament laws are the foundation from which all other laws in the world are written, therefore, we should understand them and apply them to life.

Dear Lord, I thank you for your laws. They guide me in the way I should go. Amen.

Righteousness – New Testament

There is therefore now no condemnation to them which are in Christ Jesus, who walk not after the flesh, but after the spirit. For the law of the Spirit of life in Christ Jesus hath made me free from the law of sin and death.

Romans 8: 1-2

Once a believer accepts Christ, he has come to an acknowledgement of the law and sin – and a righteous God who has power over it all.

The Bible says we are to be a righteous people (1 John 3: 10).

In fact, we are warned that our righteousness should exceed the righteousness of the scribes and Pharisees (Matthew 5: 20).

Yet Christ acknowledged disobeying the law when he healed a man's paralyzed hand on the Sabbath day (Luke 6: 6-10).

Christ said in response to his accusers, "Is it lawful on the Sabbath days to do well, or to do evil; to save life, or destroy it?"

So there's always opportunity to have the law changed.

In fact, Christians are encouraged to establish the law (Romans 3: 31).

For the cleansing of sin, Christ knew the religious law of animal sacrifices offerings could not completely redeem a person, so he fulfilled God's purpose of providing his body for the sacrifice, once, and for all the people (Hebrew 10: 10).

Dear Father, I thank you for the law which helps guide me and protect me, but I also thank You for Jesus, who died for my sin and frees me to serve you. Amen.

Safety – Old Testament

And when the morning arose, the angels' hastened Lot, saying, Arise, take thy wife, and thy two daughters, the Lord being merciful unto him and they brought him forth, and set him without the city.
Genesis 19: 16

The town of Sodom was going to be destroyed because of wickedness, so God sent two angels to help Lot and his family escape.

The Bible says, the angel of the Lord encampeth round about those who fear him, and delivereth them (Psalms 34: 7).

But stubborn Lot took his time getting out of the house, and the angels had to grab him to take him away.

When God shows us the way for safety, we should obediently follow.

Lot then complained about going to a mountain the angels said was safe.

Maybe it was too far away, or maybe his family was too tired, but God again had mercy and allowed Lot and family to stop at the town of Zoar.

Thanks to God, Lot and his family were saved from the town's burning fire except for Lot's wife who disobeyed the angel's command not to look back at the burning city as she fled the area; and then she turned into a pillar of salt.

Be not wise in thine own eyes; fear the Lord, and depart from evil (Proverbs 3: 7).

Dear Lord, You are my true refuge, and I turn to you for being safe. Have mercy up on me, my friends, and my family. Amen.

Safety – New Testament

> For whosoever shall call upon the name of the Lord shall be saved.
> Romans 10: 13

One night I had to call on the Lord for safety when a terrible fight broke out among the troops on the bridge to the Army compound in Korea where I was stationed.

Soldiers were beating each other with sticks.

I had no intention of fighting because I was leaving the country in a few weeks to go back home, so I found the back seat of a pickup truck in a dark parking lot and waited for the rampage to stop.

But there are other times to sit still and trust God.

A year earlier, I had been sitting in a chair in a recreation room at an Army base with friends watching television when an armed man came in and requested everyone to stand up and empty their pockets.

I again prayed for God's safety and looked toward the window for an escape route.

As it turned out, the man was joking, but it was a joke that could have turned deadly because war veterans in the room were ready to act.

God is our refuge and fortress, and a present help in time of trouble.

Dear Lord, I trust you to keep me safe. And I trust in Christ, who died for my sins for eternal security. Amen.

Salvation – Old Testament

Truly my soul waiteth upon God; from Him only cometh my salvation.
Psalms 62: 1

Another meaning for the word "waiteth" in the Hebrew language is "silence".

Only to God in silence is my soul; from Him only comes my salvation.

And remember, it was only after the biblical character Job became silent did God reveal Himself and grant salvation (Job 31: 40-42: 5).

Two people can not carry on a dialogue at the same time because there is confusion, so if you really want salvation, quiet yourself, and listen to God.

That means separating yourself from worldly distractions, problems, and people.

Upon confession of sin, forgiveness by God, and a commitment to serve God, there is salvation.

"Salvation belongeth unto the Lord: thy blessing is upon thy people. Hear me when I call, O God of my righteousness: thou hast enlarged me when I was in distress; have mercy upon me, and hear my prayer" (Psalms 3: 8-4: 1). Amen.

Salvation – New Testament

That if thou shalt confess with the mouth the Lord Jesus, and shalt believe in thine heart that God hath raised him from the dead, thou shalt be saved.
Romans 10: 9

Salvation is available to anyone who calls on the name of the Lord, confesses sin, and accepts Jesus as Savior (Romans 10: 11-21).

But first, the soul must become burdened to want salvation. And the Bible says to bring forth fruits worthy of repentance (Luke 3: 8).

The sinful rich man Zaccheus received salvation when he let Jesus into his home, and Jesus said, "This day is salvation come to this house" (Luke 19: 9).

Consider accepting Jesus into your life and house.

Christ says, "Behold, I stand at the door, and knock: if any man hear my voice, and open the door, I will come in to him, and will sup with him, and he with me" (Revelation 3: 20).

God is able to give us salvation through Jesus because Jesus was a holy offering for sin.

Dear Lord, I praise you for providing Jesus Christ to take away my sin and give me salvation. Amen.

Secrets – Old Testament

For thou didst it secretly, but I will do this thing before all Israel, and before the sun.
2 Samuel 12: 12

Not only was God going to expose David's sin of adultery with Bathsheba before the local people but all over the land, because David was king over all the people.

David not only secretly lay with Bathsheba but ordered her husband to the front line of a battlefield to be killed.

How evil can the heart of man be!

But David gives us a good example.

God knows all our secrets, and whether they are good or evil. In this drama, God sent Nathan the prophet to confront David about his sin.

If our secrets are good, He may conceal the matter for His glory, such as Joseph withholding his identity from his brothers so they would have grain in time of famine (Genesis 42: 7-9). And Abraham withheld his identity about being Sarah's husband from King Abimelech to save their lives.

But if our secrets are evil, He will expose the matter, because He loves us enough to correct us and put us on the right path.

The Bible says: Thou hast set our iniquities before thee, our secret sins in the light of thy countenance (Psalms 90: 8).

Dear Lord, There is nothing hidden before you. I confess my secret sins and agree to live an open righteous life. Amen.

Secrets – New Testament

"For nothing is secret that shall not be made manifest, neither anything hid, that shall not be known and come abroad."
Luke 8: 17

Jesus is talking about the glory of God and how it will not be hidden, such as a lamp that lights a room so people can see (John 8: 16).

The gift that God gives in Jesus should be no secret, and it should be openly proclaimed to the world that God has sent a Savior into the world to redeem sin.

But some secrets are to be revealed in God's time, such as when Christ's mother Mary kept the sayings of the shepherds in her heart about her baby Jesus being Savior (Luke 2: 6-19). (King Herod was seeking to kill infant children; Matthew 2: 16.)

After finding Christ, the Apostle Paul writes to the Laodiceans: For ye were once darkness, but now are ye light in the Lord; walk as children of light . . . and have no fellowship with the unfruitful works of darkness, but rather, reprove them (Ephesians 5: 8-11).

There aren't any covert secrets for the believer, because God wants the word of life spread around the world so people will know Jesus.

Jesus said nothing in secret (John 18: 20).

Dear Lord, I praise you for taking away my secret sins by confession and the acceptance of Jesus. Now I can live openly and share the gospel that frees other people. Amen.

Sex Relations (married) – Old Testament

And God blessed them, and God said unto them, "Be fruitful, and multiply . . . ."
                                                    Genesis 1: 28

Adam and Eve got together to reproduce but it was only after being disciplined by God in the Garden of Eden.

(Eve had been deceived by the devil but now accepted Adam's strength and leadership. Adam was apart from Eve but now became sensitive to her emotions and location.)

And they had children.

The Book of Solomon gives a fine example of physical intimacy between a man and a woman.

The Shulamite bride speaks of her beloved, "My beloved is mine, and I am his: he feedeth among the lilies. Until the day break, and the shadows flee away, turn, my beloved, and be thou like a roe or a young hart upon the mountain of Bether" (Song of Solomon 2: 16-17).

And the bridegroom adores his bride: "How fair is thy love, my sister, my spouse! How much better is thy love than wine! And the smell of thine ointments than all spices!" (Song of Solomon 4: 10).

Dear Lord, I praise you for my mate. May we nurture each other to enjoy the blessings that come from a commitment and love for you. Amen.

Sex Relations (married) – New Testament

Let the husband render unto the wife due benevolence: and likewise also the wife unto the husband. The wife hath not power of her own body, but the husband: and likewise also the husband hath not power of his own body, but the wife.
1 Corinthians 7: 3-4

Each person yields to the other's needs for a perfect marriage.

But when one person becomes selfish, there is a problem, which the Apostle Paul addresses: Defraud ye not one the other, except it be with consent for a time, that ye may give yourselves to fasting and prayer; and come together again, that Satan tempt you not for your incontinency (verse 5).

The Book of Ephesians helps keep physical intimacy in the right place: Husbands, love your wives, even as Christ also loved the church, and gave himself for it (Ephesians 5: 25). Wives submit yourselves unto your own husbands as unto the Lord (Ephesians 5: 22).

Men are to be reminded to give honor unto the wife as unto the weaker vessel (1 Peter 3: 7).

Marriage is honorable in all, and the bed undefiled (Hebrews 13: 4).

Dear Father in Heaven, Thank you so much for my spouse. May I be sensitive to my mate's needs and you in the spirit. Amen.

Sex Relations (unmarried)—Old Testament

And it came to pass after these things, that his master's wife cast her eyes upon Joseph; and she said, "Lie with me."

Genesis 39: 6

The master's wife was trying to entice Joseph into committing adultery but Joseph invoked God's name for help.

"How then can I do this great wickedness and sin against God?" Joseph exclaimed.

When there is a temptation to sin and have an illicit sexual relation, consider invoking God's name for separation and safety.

God is a holy God who wants all our attention on Him rather than another person.

The Bible advises a man to stay away from a strange woman (Proverbs 7: 5); lust not after her beauty in thine heart; neither let her take thee with her eyelids (Proverbs 6: 25).

If a man does have relations with a woman who is not married, he shall surely endow her to be his wife (Exodus 22: 16).

God's laws concerning improper sexual relations with people or animals are in the Book of Leviticus in Chapters 18-20.

Dear Lord, Thank you for your Word here that guides me. May I look to please you rather than the lust of the flesh. Amen.

Sex Relations (unmarried) – New Testament

This I say then, "Walk in the Spirit, and ye shall not fulfill the lust of the flesh".
Galatians 5: 16

Walking in the spirit focuses on peace, humbleness, grace, and righteousness.

But our bodies do have needs, for they were created to reproduce.

And so we are advised to let every man have his own wife; and let every woman have her own husband (1 Corinthians 7: 2); for it is better to marry than to burn (1 Corinthians 7: 9).

If intimate relations do occur outside of God's blessing, there will be discipline.

To avoid fornication, the Bible says it is not good for a man to touch a woman (1 Corinthians 7: 1);

In a time of lust, consider calling on God's Son Jesus for help, because they that are Christ's have crucified the flesh with the affection and lusts (Galatians 5: 24).

Dear Lord, I praise you for Christ who has power over the lust of the flesh. I will serve you in the spirit of life that gives you glory. Amen.

Sickness – Old Testament

And the Lord will take away from thee all sickness . . . .
Deuteronomy 7: 15

The Lord takes away sicknesses by obedience to His commandments according to the Book of Deuteronomy.

But many of us think going to a doctor, taking drugs, or learning psychology will make us well.

Only a pure and holy God can heal, and the purging of sin begins the healing process.

Consider reading also Isaiah 56-58 to show you can separate yourself to God and become a whole person free of disease.

In Isaiah's time, prideful King Hezekiah was sick unto death; but Hezekiah's sins were cast away (Isaiah 38: 17), and he was made whole.

Hezekiah also used a natural remedy of boiled figs (2 Kings 20: 7). God saw Hezekiah's tears, heard his prayer, and extended his life by fifteen years.

The true God says, "I wound, and I heal" (Deuteronomy 32: 39).

But it's up to us to want God's healing by being faithful and obedient to the commandments.

Dear Lord, I thank you for showing me how to become well by separating myself to you in complete obedience. I trust only you and your provisions to make me well. Amen.

Sickness – New Testament

For we have not a high priest which cannot be touched with the feeling of our infirmities; but was in all points tempted like as we are yet without sin. Let us therefore come boldly unto the throne of grace, that we may obtain mercy, and find grace in time of need.
Hebrews 4: 14-16

Christ can heal us because he is holy and sits on the right hand of God.

Upon confession of sin and acceptance of Christ, our sins are purged and removed by Christ's death on the cross.

Such was the man in Luke 5:18-26 sick with the palsy and could not walk, but the man must have confessed his sins, because Jesus told him his sins were forgiven.

And the man took up his bed and walked.

A woman, who had an issue of blood for twelve years that no doctor could heal, reached out and touched Jesus and was made whole (Mark 5: 25-34). Touching Jesus in the heavens makes us whole.

When infection comes, look to Christ for purity. When wounded, look to Christ to bind up. And when apathy comes, look to Christ for strength and resurrection.

The Bible says: And the prayer of faith shall save the sick, and the Lord shall raise him up; and if he hath committed sins, they shall be forgiven him. Confess your faults one to another, and pray for one another, that ye may be healed . . . (James 5:15-16).

Dear Lord, I humble myself before you and praise you for Jesus Christ who takes away my sin and can heal me. Grant me the strength I need to glorify and be healed. Amen.

Sin – Old Testament

And Achan answered Joshua, and said, "Indeed, I have sinned against the Lord god of Israel, and thus and thus have I done".
Joshua 7: 20

The soldier Achan had sinned by taking some of the goods at the battle of Jericho which God had forbidden.

Because of this sin, Israel was defeated in the next battle.

That's what sin does: it affects the whole community.

Commander Joshua knew something was wrong, so he called all the families and questioned them about coveting goods from the battle where they were ordered to not take any of the goods.

Upon interrogation, Achan's hidden goods and sin were discovered.

A psalmist's prayer helps us to avoid future sin: Keep back thy servant also from presumptuous sins; let them not have dominion over me . . . (Psalm 19: 13).

We might also take Solomon's advice in the Book of Proverbs: He that covereth his sins shall not prosper but whoso confesseth and forsaketh them, shall have mercy (Proverbs 28: 13).

Dear Lord, I am sorry that I have sinned. Please take away my sins and grant me mercy. I am willing to recompense that which I have trespassed. Amen.

Sin – New Testament

What shall we say then? Is the law sin? Nay, I had not known sin but by the law; for I had not known lust, except the law had said, Thou shalt not covet.
Romans 7: 7

The law convicts the conscience of sin, and fortunately, we have Jesus who can take away sin (Romans 2).

Jesus says, "Wherefore, I say unto you, all manner of sin and blasphemy shall be forgiven men; but the blasphemy against the Holy Spirit shall not be forgiven men" (Matthew 12: 31).

It only takes our acknowledgement, remorsefulness, petition, and the acceptance of Jesus as a sacrifice for sin.

If we say we have no sin, we make a God a liar (1 John 1: 10). All men have sinned and have come short of the glory of God (Romans 3: 23).

But it helps us to know that even if we sin, God loves us with correction.

Now, no chastening for the present seemeth to be joyous; but grievous; nevertheless, afterward it yieldeth the peaceable fruit of righteousness unto them who are corrected by it (Hebrews 12: 11).

Dear Lord, I acknowledge my sin. Have mercy on me by Christ Jesus who died for my sin. Forgive me and I shall be forgiven and I will testify of your salvation and mercy forever. Amen.

Sports – Old Testament

And Samson went and caught three hundred foxes, and took torches, and turned tail to tail, and put a torch in the midst between two tails.
Judges 15: 4

Samson was quite an entertainer tying the tails of foxes together with a firebrand and letting them run through the fields of the Philistines setting them on fire.

But he could also get serious with his sporting talent, using the jawbone of an ass to slay one thousand Philistines.

He started playing with a harlot named Delilah, who found his weakness, and the Philistines jailed Sampson, put his eyes out, and then used him in the sporting arena (Judges 16: 25-27).

Nevertheless, Sampson used his ability for the glory of God, pulling down the pillars of a stadium where the Philistines lords were entertaining themselves and worshipping their god, Dagon.

God has said, Thou shalt have no other god's before me (Exodus 20: 3). And that would include balls, goal posts, nets, and fences. We are not to bow down nor worship false gods who can not think, see, nor hear (Exodus 20: 5; Daniel 5: 23).

God is our true bread for life, and we should focus on serving him in the spirit.

Dear Father in Heaven, May this body be used for your humble service. I bow and worship you in holiness and truth. Amen.

Sports – New Testament

Know ye not that they who run in a race run all, but one receiveth the prize? So run, that ye may obtain. Now every man that striveth for the mastery is temperate in all things. Now they do it to obtain a corruptible crown, but we, an incorruptible.
1 Corinthians 9: 24-25

Receiving a trophy in sports competition for successfully finishing above other competitors is a great feeling, but receiving a crown of glory from God through Jesus Christ for the gift of eternal life is the best prize of all: it never deteriorates.

Our bodies are to be used for God's glory (1 Corinthians 6: 19-20).

Constructing housing for the homeless, cooking for the hungry, and transporting the disabled are just a few of the ways to witness and work for God, but if we are sporting them for personal recognition, we are not glorifying God.

God may cause us to suffer injury or defeat to know that He is God.

The Bible says: For bodily exercise profiteth little: but godliness is profitable unto all things . . . (1Timothy 4: 8).

Dear Lord, May my body be used for your purpose and glory. Have mercy upon me I pray. Amen.

Strength – Old Testament

And Samson lay till midnight, and arose at midnight, and took the doors of the gate of the city, and the two posts, and went away with them, bar and all, and put them upon his shoulders, and carried them up to the top of a hill that is before Hebron.   **Judges 16: 3**

Samson was a physically strong man carrying the front gate materials up a hill. He had also torn a lion in pieces, caught 300 foxes, and slayed a thousand Philistines.

But spiritually, Samson was weak.

When he told his girlfriend Delilah the secret of his strength, she told the lords of the Philistines, and they hired men to come and shave Samson's holy hair to take away his strength. (Samson was a Nazarene who vowed not to cut his hair; Numbers 6: 1.) And then Samson was imprisoned.

The Bible says, Seek the Lord and His strength: seek His face evermore (Psalms 105: 4).

Be reminded there was not one feeble person among the Israelites who came into the land of God's promise (Psalms 105: 37). They were a strong people.

By God, we receive strength (Psalms 68: 34-35), but if we have turned away from God, we are weak.

Confessing our sins and coming into agreement with God will nourish us back to strength.

We are further advised: if thou faint in the day of adversity, thy strength is small (Proverbs 24: 10

Dear Lord, Feed me the food which makes me strong, yet feed me your word of truth which makes me wise unto salvation and life. Amen.

Strength – New Testament

I can do all things with Christ who strengtheneth me.

Philippians 4: 13

Christ gives us strength because takes away the sins that burden our souls.

But we all get physically weak at times.

When Christ preached a sermon on the mountain, he felt compassion for the people who had traveled far to listen to him.

So he had his disciples gather up bread and fishes to distribute among the people for food (Mark 8: 2).

The Apostle Paul said he would rather be weak because it brought him to closer to God: Therefore, I take pleasure in infirmities, in reproaches, in necessities, in persecutions, in distresses for Christ's sake: for when I am weak, then am I strong (2 Corinthians 12: 9-10).

The Apostle is referring to leaning on God and not unto his personal understanding.

In addition, we are encouraged: Finally, my brethren, be strong in the Lord and in the power of his might. Put on the whole armor of God, that ye may be able to stand against the wiles of the devil (Ephesians 6: 10 -11).

Dear Father in Heaven. I thank you for the strength in Christ Jesus who is raised from the dead and inspires me to become strong. I also thank you for removing a burden of sin by my confession and humbleness. Amen.

Stress – Old Testament

And it came to pass on the morrow that Moses sat to judge the people: and the people stood by Moses from the morning to evening.
Exodus 18: 13

Moses was experiencing a lot of stress judging the affairs of the people, so his father-in-law Jethro gave him some good advice: Be thou for the people to God-ward, that thou mayest bring the causes unto God (Exodus 18: 19).

That's what we need to do: look Godward.

But Jethro also suggested that Moses appoint some judges over the people.

Moses listened to Jethro and took his advice; for he appointed rulers of thousands, rulers of hundreds, rulers of fifties, and rulers of tens of people.

But many of us are stubborn and think no one else can do a job; so it takes a serious sickness to finally get our attention.

Before it gets to that time, consider involving God in decision making.

Consider also reading Psalm 107 which shows the children of Israel suffering from stress: they were overworked, wandering, confused, and sinful; yet the psalmist extolled God's goodness and mercy.

Dear Lord, Have mercy on me and forgive me for being so prideful. You are my first desire, and I lay down my pride to accept your will and rest for my life. Amen.

Stress – New Testament

"Come unto me, all ye that labor and are heavy laden, and I will give you rest. Take my yoke upon you, and learn of me: for I am meek and lowly in heart: and ye shall find rest unto your souls. For my yoke is easy, and my burden is light."
Matthew 11: 28-30

Jesus had a light burden because he had no sin.

And his yoke was easy because it was attached to his Father in Heaven who gave him grace and comfort.

Comfort from God is available to anyone who gives up selfish ambitions and rests in the Lord's grace.

Pride, selfishness, and fighting are all given up.

This doesn't mean to stop working entirely but to rely on God's work rather than selfish works -- to enter the privilege of trusting God for life.

Consider the man Jesus who made himself of no reputation and took upon him the form of a servant (Philippians 2: 7).

He gives us rest from stress and freedom from sin, by belief and faith.

Dear Lord, I praise you for Jesus who takes away my sin to give me rest. Have mercy upon me I pray. Amen.

Suicide – Old Testament

"I call heaven and earth to record this day against you, that I have set before you life and death, blessing and cursing; therefore, choose life, and that both thou and thy seed may live."
Deuteronomy 30: 19

These words were spoken by Moses to the people just before his death.

God often puts a choice of life or death before people today.

If life and goodness are chosen, then there is testimony of God's saving presence and glory, but if death and evil are chosen, God cannot be praised from the grave (Psalms 6: 5; 88: 10).

God commands us not to kill (Exodus 20: 13), and that includes us as well as other people.

If the words of Moses didn't put God's fear into the people, maybe Joshua's did because he made a similar speech, "And if seem evil to you to serve the Lord, choose you this day whom ye will serve" (Joshua 24: 15).

The people responded, "The Lord our God will we serve, and his voice will we obey" (Joshua 24: 24).

Dear Lord, "For thou hast delivered my soul from death; mine eyes from tears, and my feet from falling. I will walk before the Lord in the land of the living" (Psalms 116: 8-9). Amen.

Suicide – New Testament

And the keeper of the prison, awaking out of his sleep and seeing the prison doors open, drew out his sword and would have killed himself, supposing that the prisoners had been fled.

The Acts 16: 27

The jailer was about to commit suicide because he would face terrible discipline when his boss found about the jail door being open and the prisoners gone.

But Paul cried with a loud voice, saying, "Do thyself no harm; for we are all here" (Acts 16: 28).

So God intervened into the jailer's life. (The disciples had also been singing hymns and praying.)

But it takes the intervention of God before we stop trying to kill ourselves, and knowing Jesus Christ has already died for us, gives us life.

The Apostle Paul thought of dying when he was troubled, yet he did not trust in himself but trusted in God who raises the dead (2 Corinthians 1: 8-9).

Christ Jesus gives us power over death (1 Corinthians 15: 54-57), and the last enemy death has been defeated.

Dear Lord, I humbly accept the risen Christ by the confession of sin into my heart and life. I am renewed in the spirit of my mind to live for you. For whosoever shall call upon the name of the Lord shall be saved (Romans 10: 13). Amen.

Terror – Old Testament

And Mount Sinai was altogether on a smoke, because the Lord descended upon it in fire: and the smoke thereof ascended as the smoke of a furnace, and the whole mount quaked greatly.

Exodus 19: 18

When the people saw the power of God, they got scared.

But their leader Moses told them to stand back, unless they wanted to get hurt – that only he and Aaron the priest would be able to approach God.

Holy men are not scared of terror because they have made peace with God, and they understand the judgments and discipline that take place.

Moses told the people God was testing their faith -- to see if they would fear Him.

When powerful events happen, look to God for safety and answers.

But he usually gives warnings about catastrophic events, such as what happened on Mount Sinai.

Man tries to imitate the power of God with bombs, noise, and chaos, but God is still in charge of terror, and he would never forego mercy on the people.

.

Dear Lord, I know you are a mighty God and worthy to be feared. Have mercy upon me as I draw close to you and seek your will. Amen.

Terror – New Testament

"For nation shall rise against nation, and kingdom against kingdom; and there shall be famines, pestilences, and earthquakes in divers places".
Matthew 24: 7

Jesus says terrible events may end the world and mankind, so he warns us to be prepared, such as five brides waiting to see their bridegroom in the dark: the brides had their oil ready to burn for the lamps to shine (Matthew 25: 1-13).

The advent of terrifying events makes us want to be prepared to meet God.

But Jesus also comforts us saying he will be in the midst of terror -- in the clouds of heaven with great power and glory (Matthew 24: 31).

So if we know Jesus, and have made peace with God, we are saved.

We are not to be scared of man's terror, who can only kill the body (1 Peter 3: 14); but we are to fear God, who can destroy body and soul in hell (Matthew 10: 28).

Take comfort in knowing there is nothing that has happened that has not happened before (1 Peter 4: 12).

And Jesus has promised to be with us to the end (Matthew 28: 20).

Dear Lord, I thank you for Jesus in my life. I know I have safety in heaven regardless of what happens in the world. Jesus has prepared a place for me. Establish peace I pray, all over the world. Amen.

Thankfulness – Old Testament

And when Abigail saw David, she hastened, and alighted from the ass, and fell before David on her face, and bowed to the ground.
1 Samuel 25: 23

Abigail was thankful David and his men had protected her land and family during a nearby war, so she made some food to show thanks.

We might do a good deed for other people to show thanks, but our offerings should also be made to God.

The Bible says, Offer unto God thanksgiving, and pay thy vows unto the Most High, and call upon me in the day of trouble; I will deliver thee, and thou shalt glorify me (Psalms 50: 14-15).

King David gave his life to God and said a lengthy prayer that thanked Him (I Chronicles 16: 7-36).

But if we do not acknowledge God, nor thank Him for mercy and forgiveness, He may not acknowledge us (2 Chronicles 15: 2).

Dear Lord, I thank you for your presence here and praise your holy name. You are good and your mercy endures forever. Amen.

Thankfulness – New Testament

Giving thanks always for all things unto God and the Father in the name of our Lord Jesus Christ.
Ephesians 5: 20

God wants our thankfulness just as we would want thanks from another person.

If we fail to praise him, we may be like the fools the Apostle Paul described in Romans 2, who were given over to vile affections.

And we are to thank Jesus. Paul thanked him for putting him into the ministry and receiving mercy (1 Timothy 1: 12-13).

But we will not always get thanks for doing good deeds, such as the servant described in Luke 17: 7-10: it is our duty to work for God.

However, *we* like to get thanks, and we are encouraged by Jesus to witness to the unsaved.

Jesus said, "For if ye love them who love you, what thanks have ye? For sinners also love those who love them. And if ye do good to them who do good to you, what thanks have ye? For sinners also do even the same" (Luke 6: 32-33).

Lonely, hungry, and desolate people love getting new friends and hearing about Jesus, and usually, they are very thankful.

Thank God for providing a Savior in the person of Jesus Christ to take away sin and grant a new life.

May we continue to give the sacrifice of praise to God continually, that is the fruit of our lips giving thanks (Hebrews 13: 15).

Dear Lord, Thank you for Jesus who died for me so that I can serve you. May I give thanks everyday in my words, tithes, and deeds. Amen.

Travel – Old Testament

" . . . For the Lord thy God is with thee whithersoever thou goest."

Joshua 1: 9

Joshua received these words from God shortly before leading the people into a strange land.

Knowing God's presence gives us courage and strength to travel into unknown territory.

But we are warned that the sight [from] the eyes is better than the wandering of the desire (Ecclesiastes 6: 9).

We can enjoy God's presence right here in prayer and fellowship.

And we are further warned: As a bird that wandereth from her nest, so is man that wandereth from his place (Proverbs 27: 8).

So it's a good idea to have someone watch home.

But if we have to travel, may we look to God for guidance.

He will lead us in righteousness and safety, but we must call on His name beforehand and trust him.

Dear Lord, I thank you for being here and in my destination. Provide me with necessary provisions and keep me safe. Amen.

Travel – New Testament

And it came to pass, afterward, that he went throughout every city and village, preaching and showing the glad tidings of the kingdom of God; and the twelve were with him.

Luke 8: 1

Jesus did a lot of traveling witnessing for God because he wanted to spread good news.

But he encountered many delays. He met people with demons and illnesses. He met lawyers who wanted to debate the law. And he met soldiers, priests, and rich people who asked about God.

We may experience such delays when traveling, but those are good times for testifying of God and Jesus.

There may even be time to perform a good deed.

Jesus would heal the sick.

There can be difficult people along the traveling trail, but the Bible says to forbear one another in love (Ephesians 4: 2; Colossians 3: 13).

May we prepare in advance for travel by acquiring necessary provisions but also gather material to witness for God and Christ.

The love for Jesus transcends all people, cultures, and places.

Dear Father, Your word of life is commissioned to be spread all over the world. May everyone know about Jesus. Have mercy on me when I travel. Amen.

Trials – Old Testament

But he knoweth the way that I take: when he hath tried me, I shall come forth as gold. My foot hath held his steps, his way have I kept, and not declined.
Job 23: 10-11

Job stayed around God's throne regardless of personal trouble.

When troubles come, and they will, don't doubt God's plan for success -- but persevere in patience to receive the promise (read Psalms 78 and 95).

Job was eventually healed of his affliction.

There have been other saints as faithful as Job.

Abraham was about to sacrifice his son on an altar, but by obedience to God, he found an animal sacrifice (Genesis 22: 1-14).

Daniel was put in a den of lions but he kept his faith in God for safety (Daniel 6: 16-23).

Life is full of trials that test our faith, but at the end of the journey, God will fulfill the promise.

My heart is fixed, O God, my heart is fixed; I will sing and give praise (Psalms 57: 7).

.

Dear Father in Heaven, I praise you for being here in my trial and saving me from sin. You have control over this situation and I praise you for keeping me humble and righteous. Amen.

Trials – New Testament

That the trial of your faith, being much more precious than of gold that perisheth, though it be tried with fire, might be found unto praise and honor and glory at the appearing of Jesus Christ.
1 Peter 1: 7

After learning about God, there are always trials that test our faith.

Jesus was faced with such trials in the desert when the devil came along and tried to convince him that stones were bread, promised to give him the kingdoms of the world, and offered him a job in the world church (Matthew 4: 3-10).

But Jesus knew his mission from God and rejected the devil's offers.

When trials come along, pray, and read the word of God for victory and patience.

The Bible says, my brethren, count it all joy when ye fall into divers temptations, knowing this, that the trying of your faith worketh patience (James 1: 2-3).

Bible concordances provide reference Scriptures for subjects related to faith testers such as alcohol, lust, debt, or immoral sex.

Researching those words and reading scriptures will show that God has victory over the temptation: we only need trust Him for victory.

Dear Lord, Thank you for Jesus, who has victory over evil. May I follow the plan you have for my life that is good and gives you the glory. Amen.

Truth – Old Testament

God is not a man that he should lie; neither the son of man that he should repent. Hath he said and shall he not do it? Or hath he spoken and shall he not make it good?

Numbers 23: 19

God can be trusted because He does not lie.

Man cannot be trusted because he is often full of deceit; therefore, we need God for truth.

Deuteronomy 32: 4 says God is the rock, his work is perfect; for all his ways are judgment; a God of truth and without iniquity, just and right is he.

And the Psalmist praised this God of truth: Thy righteousness is an everlasting righteousness, and thy law is the truth (Psalms 119: 142).

King David's prayer helps us: Lead me in thy truth, teach me, for thou art the God of my salvation, on thee do I wait all the day (Psalms 25: 5).

God has provided us truth in the Holy Scripture.

All the paths of the Lord are mercy and truth unto such as keep his covenant and his testimonies (Psalm 25: 10).

Dear Lord, I thank you for providing your record of truth in the Old Testament. Your word is truly a lamp unto my feet and a light unto my path. Amen.

Truth – New Testament

Jesus saith unto him, "I am the way, the truth, and the life . . . ."
John 14: 6

Truth records in the New Testament that the Gentiles needed a Savior, so God sent His son Jesus in the form of a man to be a sacrifice for sin.

This sin sacrifice could only come by a sinless man, so Jesus was born of a virgin woman.

He died for the people's sins and rose into heaven on the third day and now intercedes on behalf of believers for comfort and peace.

Men who refuse the teachings and acceptance of Christ as Savior are referred to as anti-Christ (1 John 4: 1-3).

Further, if we say we have not sinned, we make God a liar; (1 John 1: 10).

According to Jesus, those who worship God are to worship in spirit and truth (John 4: 24); but Jesus also says, "No man cometh to the Father but by me" (John 14: 6).

Upon confession of Jesus, God sends us the Spirit of truth and comforts us with the Holy Spirit (John 14: 17; 15-26-27; 16: 13).

Dear Lord, I praise you for the truth that comes by Jesus. Forgive my sins and sanctify me by this truth. Amen.

War – Old Testament

The Lord is a mighty warrior; the Lord is his name
                                                    Exodus 15: 3

God warred to deliver his people from slavery and get his glory in another land as pursuing Egyptians were drowned in the waters of the Red Sea.

God fights for us when we are obedient to the commandments and give him glory.

But many of us war for personal land, money, and natural resources.

We are warned in God's law not to covet anything from a neighbor (Exodus 20:17), nor oppress strangers (Exodus 22: 21).

Consider Proverbs 24: 6: For by wise counsel thou shalt make thy war, and in the multitude of counselors, there is safety.

Usually the war is within ourselves: one part of us wants to do one thing while the other wants to do something else.

May we humble ourselves from personal war to know that God is always victorious.

God creates war, but He also makes war to cease (Psalms 46: 9).

Dear Lord, You are in charge of war, and your righteousness and glory will prevail. May we be spared of violence to worship and love you. Amen.

War -- New Testament

Then said Jesus unto him, "Put up again thy sword into its place; for all they that take up the sword perish by the sword."
Matthew 26: 52

Christ gives us wisdom by saying if we use weapons, they will be used against us.

But Christ does make war.

According to the author of the Book of Revelation, he wars from heaven in righteousness (Revelation 19: 11).

And the soldier Saul became a victim of Christ when he was riding down the road and brought to a stop (Acts 9: 1-20).

Christ asked Saul why he was *persecuting him,* and when Saul questioned Christ's identity, he was struck and disabled.

Humiliated, Saul was led into the city of Damascus where he received instructions from the disciple Ananias to go and preach about Jesus.

The war continues to spread the good news about Jesus.

For he is our peace, who hath made both one, and hath broken down the middle wall of partition between us (Ephesians 2: 14).

Dear Lord, Thank you for Jesus who has overcome the lust of the flesh and the war within us. He allows us to love all of humanity. May I refrain from arguing and fighting and seek this peace that passes all understanding. Amen.

Wisdom – Old Testament

The fear of the Lord is the beginning of wisdom, but fools despise knowledge and instruction.
Proverbs 1: 7

Fearing God is the beginning of wisdom because He has power over our souls.

Understanding he is our Creator puts us in the right place to learn, for with the lowly is wisdom (Proverbs 11: 2).

Consider some meek and lowly men in the Bible who had wisdom: Moses, Joseph, Job, and Daniel.

Their lowly demeanor gave them access to God's heightened wisdom.

The wisdom books of the Bible are considered to be Job, Psalms, Proverbs, Ecclesiastes, and the Song of Solomon. The characteristics of wisdom are listed in Proverbs Chapters 1-9.

God's wisdom saved Abraham from Melchizedek's army, got Joseph out of jail, taught Jacob to multiply cattle, showed Noah how to build an ark, and showed Nehemiah and friends how to rebuild temple walls.

We are encouraged to seek wisdom while it may be found; otherwise, we are warned, God may not answer us when anguish and distress comes (Proverbs 1; 24-32).

Dear Lord, You are my wisdom, and I humble myself from my own wisdom to listen to you for discernment, prosperity, and safety. Amen.

Wisdom – New Testament

For the wisdom of this world is foolishness with God. For it is written, He taketh the wise in their own craftiness.
1 Corinthians 3: 19

Man would have you believe wisdom comes from worldly textbooks and personal thought, but the Lord knoweth the thoughts of the wise, that they are vain (1 Corinthians 3: 20). And the wisdom of this world is earthly, sensual, and devilish (James 3: 15).

The mystery of receiving great wisdom is explained in the 2nd Chapter of 1 Corinthians: Now we have received not the spirit of the world, but the spirit which is of God (1 Corinthians 2: 12).

The Bible says: If any of you lack wisdom, let him ask of God, that giveth to all men liberally, and upbraideth not; and it shall be given him (James 1: 5). The wisdom that comes from above is first pure, then peaceable . . . (James 3: 17).

This is the wisdom we need, which gives peace.

The secret to getting wisdom is becoming lowly and dependent on God, and it usually takes a humiliating experience to find it.

The greatest wisdom we can have is that which grants personal salvation (2 Timothy 3: 15).

Dear Lord, I thank you for wisdom in the Holy Scriptures. Wisdom shows me how to live and receive your blessings, but the greatest wisdom I can have is receiving your Son Jesus who saves my soul. Amen.

Work – Old Testament

And the Lord took the man, and put him into the garden of Eden, to dress it, and to till it.
Genesis 2: 15

Man was put on earth to work and glorify God, but he was then condemned to work by the sweat of his face for disobeying the instructions (Genesis 3: 17-19).

Nevertheless, the Bible says it is a gift from God to work: There is nothing better for a man . . . that he should make his soul enjoy good in his labor (Ecclesiastes 2:24).

But the first work we should do is study and understand God's law, ordinances, and commandments; then we know who and what we are working for.

Otherwise, we will be enslaved to another god (read Deuteronomy 4: 23-28).

If we don't want to work, the Bible says we will hunger (Proverbs 19: 15).

The Book of Proverbs gives us some wisdom: Labor not to be rich; cease from thine own wisdom (Proverbs 23: 4).

But in all labor, there is profit (Proverbs 14: 23).

Dear Lord, I praise you for letting me work. Complete the work that you have begun in me to produce good things, and may all this work glorify you. Amen.

Work – New Testament

"Labor not for the food which perisheth but for that food which endureth to everlasting life, which the Son of man shall give unto you; for him hath God the Father sealed."

John 6: 27

Christ advises us to work for those things which give everlasting life.

When we are pleasing God with work, then daily provisions will take care of themselves.

For example, when seventy servants went out to work and spread the good news of salvation, they carried neither purse, money, or shoes; yet they were sustained with daily provisions and returned with joy (Luke 10: 4-17).

But the disciples also asked, "What shall we do, that we might work the works of God?"

Jesus answered and said unto them, "This is the work of God, that ye might believe on him whom he hath sent" (John 6: 29).

Believing in Jesus gives us access to God works: we have the power of healing, teaching, nursing, ministering, constructing, and miracles.

Dear Lord, I praise you for showing me the work you want me to do. Perfect that which concerns me and may your work prosper. Amen.

Worry – Old Testament

God is our refuge and strength, a very present help in trouble. Therefore will not we fear; though the earth be removed, and the mountains carried into the midst of the sea.
Psalms 46: 1-2

Psalm 46 comforts us because it shows God is in control of what happens on earth.

But there is more wisdom from the scriptures to relieve us: we are not to worry about tomorrow (Proverbs 27: 1); we are not to worry about the weather (Ecclesiastes 11: 4); and we are not to worry about wars in other countries (Psalms 66: 7).

But we have plenty to worry about if we are separated from God, because his discipline can be harsh.

The sinner David said of his sin, "I am troubled; I am bowed down greatly; I go mourning all the day long" (Psalm 38: 6).

We do not want to be troubled like David, so let's make sure sin is confessed, for peace with God.

And then we can have mercy and life (Proverbs 28: 15).

The Psalmist finishes Psalm 46 saying: Be still, and know that I am God; I will be exalted among the nations, I will be exalted in the earth. The Lord of hosts is with us; the God of Jacob is our refuge. Selah.

Dear Lord, With you, I can face this anxiety and feel calm. May I patiently seek this cause for worry and have it removed, for I am saved by faith and trust in you. Amen.

Worry – New Testament

"Therefore, take no thought saying: What shall we eat? Or what shall we drink? Or with what shall we be clothed?"
Matthew 6: 31

Much of our worry is about food, drink, or clothing, but Jesus says not to worry: seek the kingdom of God and His righteousness, and daily provisions will be given to us.

But other events such as nearby wars, technological hazards, pollution, crime, monetary debt, and illness may cause us to worry: because they affect our mental and physical health.

But God has control over these issues, for the world is subject to God (Revelation 14: 7).

So Jesus advises us to watch and pray (Matthew 24: 42).

The Apostle Paul gives some advice by saying: to be {anxious} for nothing, but in everything, by prayer and supplication with thanksgiving, let your requests be made known unto God (Philippians 4: 6).

And the peace of God, which passeth all understanding, shall keep your hearts and mind through Christ Jesus (verse 7).

Dear Lord, Thank you for increasing my faith. I know that you are in control of this situation and I look to you for the right thing to do. Amen.

Worship – Old Testament

Thou shalt have no other gods before me. Thou shalt not make unto thee any graven image, or any likeness of anything that is in heaven above, or that is in the earth beneath, or that is in the water under the earth; Thou shalt not bow down thyself to them, nor serve them . . . .   Exodus 20: 3-5

This first commandment tells us God has priority over all other gods.

But this God is also able to forgive and redeem sin, grant prosperity or poverty, and provide blessings or curses.

So He wants worship, and we are commanded to love Him with all [our] heart, and with all [our] soul, and with all [our] might (Deuteronomy 6: 5).

Psalms 95 exhorts us to worship: O come, let us worship and bow down: let us kneel before the Lord our maker. For He is our God; and we are the sheep of His pasture . . . (verse 5-6).

But in order to worship this God, we have to put away false idols, worldly distractions, and personal sin.

When the patriarch Jacob and company went to worship God at Bethel, they were to put away their strange gods and get cleaned up (Genesis 35).

That's what we need to do: put away strange gods and get cleaned up. God is holy, and we are to be holy with Him. And wherever God wants us to worship, we are to worship Him in spirit and truth.

Dear Lord, My praise shall be of Thee in the great congregation: I will pay my vows before them that fear him. The meek shall eat and be satisfied: they shall praise the Lord that seek him; your heart shall live for ever; (Psalms 22: 25-26). Amen.

Worship – New Testament

"Blessing, and honor, and glory, and power be unto him that sitteth upon the throne and unto the Lamb forever and ever."
Revelation 5: 13

Jesus is worthy to be worshipped because he is the Son of God who arose from the dead and gives us victory over the fear of sin and death.

He sits in the heavens on the right hand of God to intercede for us.

The Bible says, but this man, because he continueth forever . . . is also able to save them to the uttermost that come unto God by him, seeing he ever liveth to make intercession for them (Hebrews 7: 24-25).

Christ is at the door to the temple of God in heaven, and if we hear his voice and open the door, he will come and dine with us (Revelation 3: 20).

He is worthy to be praised for giving us life.

Dear Lord, I praise you for Jesus in the congregation of saints. You have provided a great sacrifice for our sins. Amen.

www.ingramcontent.com/pod-product-compliance
Lightning Source LLC
Chambersburg PA
CBHW032134040426
42449CB00005B/236